40 HADITH FROM

Sahih Muslim

SHAHRUL HUSSAIN
& ZAHED FETTAH

Forty Hadith from Sahih Muslim

First Published in 2023 by
THE ISLAMIC FOUNDATION

Distributed by
KUBE PUBLISHING LTD
Tel +44 (0)1530 249230
E-mail: info@kubepublishing.com
Website: www.kubepublishing.com

Author Shahrul Hussain & Zahed Fettah
Editor Umm Marwan Ibrahim
Cover Design Afreen Fazil (Jaryah Studios)
Arabic/English layout & design Nasir Cadir

A Cataloguing-in-Publication Data record for this book
is available from the British Library

ISBN 978-0-86037-945-4
eISBN 978-0-86037-950-8

Printed by Elma Basim, Turkey

Dedication

For Br Rizvan Khalid and his family

Contents

	Introduction	vii
	Acknowledgments	x
	A Brief Biography of Imam Muslim	xi
Hadith 1	What Makes Allah Happy	1
Hadith 2	Honesty is the Best Policy	3
Hadith 3	The Tricks of Dajjāl (Anti-Christ)	5
Hadith 4	Signs of the Day of Judgement	8
Hadith 5	Help Yourself after Your Death	11
Hadith 6	Setting a Good Example	14
Hadith 7	Beware of Backbiting	16
Hadith 8	It is Important to Have a Good Name	19
Hadith 9	Knock Knock! Who's there?	21
Hadith 10	Private Chit-chat in Front of Others	23
Hadith 11	Meaning of Good Dreams and Bad Dreams	25
Hadith 12	Voluntary Prayers at Home	28
Hadith 13	Zero Tolerance to Weapons	30
Hadith 14	Three Deadly Sins	32
Hadith 15	Never Fall for the Same Trick Twice	35
Hadith 16	The Clear Sign of Faith	37
Hadith 17	Collective Worship	39
Hadith 18	All Intoxicants are Unlawful	43
Hadith 19	Torture is Unlawful in Islam	45
Hadith 20	You are What You Eat	48

Hadith 21	Seven Things to do and Seven Things not to do	51
Hadith 22	Criticising Food	55
Hadith 23	Returning Lost and Found Property	58
Hadith 24	Only Allah's Name Should be Taken for an Oath	61
Hadith 25	Bequests Cannot be More Than One-third	64
Hadith 26	Taking Back a Gift	67
Hadith 27	Writing off Half the Debt	70
Hadith 28	How to Wash the Dead: Death During Hajj	73
Hadith 29	An Easy Way to Get the Reward of Reading One-third of the Qur'an	76
Hadith 30	The Virtues of Praying at a Mosque	79
Hadith 31	Women Attending Mosques	82
Hadith 32	Taking a Bath When it's Cold	85
Hadith 33	Spending Money	88
Hadith 34	Fasting While Travelling	91
Hadith 35	How to Behave While Fasting	93
Hadith 36	The Virtue of Ashura	96
Hadith 37	A Bad Haircut	99
Hadith 38	Breastfeeding a Child	101
Hadith 39	The Rights of a Business Partner	104
Hadith 40	Leaving the Mosque after the Call to Prayer	106

Introduction

All praise is due to Allah, the Lord of the universe, the Most Merciful the Most Kind, the Master of the Day of Judgement. Peace and blessings be upon Muhammad ﷺ, the final Prophet of Allah, and upon his family and Companions.

Hadith is one of the most important institutions in Islam. It contains the teachings of the Prophet Muhammad ﷺ regarding all aspects of Islam. It is indispensable in order to attain the correct understanding of the religion, and without it, guidance is not possible. Therefore, it is essential for all Muslims to make an effort to understand and study Hadith, even if it is at a basic level.

Unfortunately, most of the works of Hadith literature available in English are long, detailed, and viewed as heavy reads by the general masses. As these are religious texts, it can be daunting for beginners to understand the subject. There are mainly two types of books about Hadith in English. While one type deals with the science of Hadith in terms of its historical phenomena as a vital Islamic institution, the other consists of thick volumes of English renditions of Hadith corpuses—both of which can put off beginners from reading and understanding Hadith.

This dilemma gave birth to the 'Forty Ahadith' project, in which we set out to compile a series of forty ahadith from each of the six canonical books of Hadith. The collection aims to educate people who wish to enjoy Hadith literature without delving too deep into its technicalities. The style and language used in these books is non-specialised and thereby accessible to readers of all levels and ages. As such, the collection is also ideal for new Muslims who wish to learn more about Hadith.

In this particular volume, we have selected forty ahadith from *Ṣaḥīḥ Muslim* in order to give the reader a flavour of the Hadith literature found within the *Ṣaḥīḥ*. There is no particular reason for choosing the ahadith mentioned herein. However, each hadith will reflect a unique theme so as to touch upon various aspects of the Islamic teachings, such as:

- Manners and Etiquettes
- Character of a Muslim
- Exhortations and Admonitions
- Remembrance of Allah
- Knowledge and Action
- Beliefs

When selecting the forty ahadith for each book in the series, we made sure to avoid lengthy and elaborate narrations or those that dealt with complex legal and theological matters. Instead, you will find that the selected ahadith focus on character, spirituality, morals, manners and ethics, and that the accompanying explanations of the ahadith focus on highlighting these aspects.

Within this volume is a simple discussion of the theoretical parameters of praiseworthy characters every Muslim should aspire to achieve, supererogatory virtuous acts of worship, and the moral philosophy (in particular normative ethics) of these ahadith. It is hoped that this will open the doors for readers to enquire more about Hadith as an important source of revelation.

Finally, it is worth pointing out that the reason for compiling forty ahadith is due to the virtuous nature of 'forty' ahadith recorded in many traditions of the Prophet Muhammad ﷺ. It is related that Prophet Muhammad ﷺ said, 'Whoever memorises forty ahadith regarding the matters of religion, Allah will resurrect him on the Day of Judgement from among the group of jurists and scholars' (*Bayhaqī*). Although this hadith is weak in its authenticity, many scholars have strongly supported acting on weak ahadith, which solely speak about virtues of good deeds, for the sake of spirituality. What is of even more benefit is to memorise forty ahadith from *Ṣaḥīḥ Muslim*. The short ahadith in this compilation may help facilitate young learners and beginners to memorise the beloved Prophet's sayings, which would be a great achievement.

We would like to conclude by thanking everyone who has made this project possible, especially Br Haris Ahmad from Kube Publishing House for his support; without his help, this project would not have been possible. The people we are most indebted to are the patrons of the Ibn Rushd Centre of Excellence for Islamic Research. This work is dedicated to them and all those who support the advancement of knowledge and research.

Shahrul Hussain & Zahed Fettah
8th April 2019 / 3rd Shaʿbān 1440

Acknowledgments

It would not be possible to accomplish this work without the support of many great people, too many to mention all of them by name. First and foremost, we thank our parents for their love and support. Our teachers for their patience and mentoring. We are most obliged to mention our heartfelt thanks to Abida Akhtar and Sumayah Ali for their invaluable feedback. A very special heartfelt thanks to Rabiya Dawood and Heba Malick for their fastidious editorial work.

The English language or indeed any other language does not afford a word to express our deepest gratitude to Br Rizvan Khalid for his support and help. We would also like to thank Sr Mahmooda Begum and Sr Samina Salim for their support and dedication in promoting reading, learning and Islamic education.

"I ask Allah to raise the rank of my parents and bless them in this life and the next, for they have encouraged me on my path of learning and seeking knowledge."

Zahed Fettah

A Brief Biography of Imam Muslim

Abū al-Ḥusayn Muslim ibn al-Ḥajjāj ibn Muslim al-Naysābūrī, famously known as Imam Muslim, was born in the year 204 AH in Nishapur, northeast of what is known today as Iran. He began seeking knowledge from an early age, studying with some of the most senior scholars of his time, including Aḥmad ibn Ḥanbal, Isḥāq ibn Rāhwayh, Qutaybah ibn Saʿīd, Muḥammad ibn Yaḥyā al-Dhuhlī, and Muḥammad ibn Ismāʿīl al-Bukhārī.

Imam Muslim was highly respected by the scholars of his time, including his own teachers. Aḥmad ibn Maslamah said, 'I saw Abū Ḥātim and Abū Zurʿah (two of the leading scholars of Hadith) consider Muslim ibn al-Ḥajjāj to have greater knowledge of authentic ahadith than all the scholars of their time.' Muḥammad ibn Bashar (a leading Hadith scholar and one of the teachers of Imam Muslim) said, 'The Hadith experts (*ḥuffāẓ*) of the world are four: Abū Zurʿah in Rayy, Muslim in Nishapur, al-Dārimī in Samarqand, and Muḥammad ibn Ismāʿīl (al-Bukhārī) in Bukhara.'

Imam Muslim authored one of the greatest works in the field of Hadith, known today as *Ṣaḥīḥ Muslim*. His masterpiece preserved most of the authentic teachings of the Prophet Muhammad ﷺ. He compiled his book by selecting from around 300,000 ahadith he heard from his teachers and summarised this into a book containing around 7,500 hadith narrations.

In the introduction of his book, he explained the main reasons for authoring the book. He mentions that someone requested him to author a book which summarised the most important authentic ahadith from the Prophet Muhammad ﷺ, in the hope that it would be an easy reference for those wishing to focus on studying the meanings of ahadith. Imam Muslim also adds that he was further encouraged to compile this book when he saw that some people were spreading false and weak reports amongst the masses.

Ṣaḥīḥ Muslim has become an essential reference for Muslims since the time of the author, and it is considered the most authentic book after *Ṣaḥīḥ al-Bukhārī*. It is easier to follow than *Ṣaḥīḥ al-Bukhārī*, because the author has collected the various narrations of the same hadith in one place, unlike Bukhārī who has dispersed them around his book according to the topic. The most relied upon commentary of *Ṣaḥīḥ Muslim* today is the one authored by Imam al-Nawawī. Imam Muslim also authored another book called *Kitāb al-Tamyīz* in which he discusses hidden defects found in some ahadith, which may appear, at first sight, sound to those who have a limited understanding of hadith defects. The book indicates his intricate knowledge of authentic and defective ahadith.

Some of the prominent Hadith scholars who studied and narrated ahadith from Imam Muslim include, al-Tirmidhī, Ibn Khuzaymah, Ibn ʿAwanah, and ʿAbd al-Raḥmān ibn Abī Ḥātim. Imam Muslim passed away in the year 261 AH in Nishapur, may Allah have mercy on him. Despite only living for around 55 years, he left behind a monumental work considered to be one of the greatest ever references of Hadith.

The Importance of Hadith and its Significance

Allah sent Messengers throughout history with the objective of clarifying the truth to the people and guiding them to Him. Many of these Messengers were also sent with Books containing guidance, such as the final Messenger of Allah, Prophet Muhammad ﷺ. He was sent to teach the Book, the Qur'an, and to be the living example of the teachings of the Qur'an. As Allah states in the Qur'an: *'Allah has surely conferred a favour on the believers when He sent in their midst a Messenger from among themselves who recites to them His verses, purifies them, and teaches them the Book and the Wisdom, while previously they had been in clear misguidance'* (*Āl 'Imrān* 3: 164). Allah also states: *'And we have sent down the Reminder (the Qur'an) to you so that you (O Messenger) may clarify to the people that which has been sent down to them, and so that they may ponder'* (*al-Naḥl* 16: 44).

These verses highlight that the role of the Messenger ﷺ is to clarify and teach the Qur'an. His words and his actions, which form a verbal and practical interpretation of the Qur'an, is the Prophetic Tradition referred to as the 'Sunnah'. Following the Sunnah is necessary because it is the only way to practice the teachings of the final Book of Allah correctly.

Allah has taken it upon Himself to preserve the Qur'an: *'It is certainly We who have revealed the Reminder, and it is certainly We who will preserve it'* (*al-Ḥijr* 15: 9). This preservation is not restricted to the letters and words of the Qur'an but also includes the preservation of its meanings, which is fulfilled through the Prophetic implementation of the Qur'an—the Sunnah.

It is simply not possible to observe the teachings of Islam without following the Sunnah. The purpose of the Qur'an is to teach us the correct belief and acts of worship Allah demands from us in order to prove our servitude to Him. It is not, however, an instruction manual detailing precise rules and methods of worshipping Allah.

Moreover, written or verbal instructions are not enough; it requires a teacher to show us the practical way of worshipping Allah. Thus, while the Qur'an outlines the commandments of Allah such as to fast, give zakat, perform hajj and the like, the role of the Prophet ﷺ is to teach us *how* to perform those acts of worship. Therefore, without knowing and following the Sunnah, Muslims will not be able to observe the teachings of the Qur'an.

Compilation of Hadith

Although the Qur'an was collected and written in one place much earlier than the Hadith, the latter was also preserved in similar ways to the former. Ahadith were written down by some Companions at the time of the Messenger ﷺ, but this habit only became widespread a century or so after his death.

Since the second century after *hijrah*, many scholars wrote down the ahadith of the Prophet ﷺ. Some scholars compiled books of Hadith which discussed the various areas of the teachings of the Prophet ﷺ. Sadly, some of the earliest books of Hadith were lost. However, some survived and were transmitted throughout centuries until our time, including the *Muwaṭṭā'* of Imam Mālik (d. 179 AH), the *Muṣannaf* of 'Abd al-Razzāq (d. 211 AH), the *Muṣannaf* of Ibn Abī Shaybah (d. 235 AH), and the *Musnad* of Imam Aḥmad ibn Ḥanbal (d. 241 AH). These books contain thousands of reports from the Prophet ﷺ and his Companions, clarifying how they implemented the Qur'anic teachings in their everyday life.

Hundreds of books of Hadith were authored, but only a dozen of them became famous and spread worldwide. The nine most relied-upon books of Hadith are:

1. *Ṣaḥīḥ al-Bukhārī*
2. *Ṣaḥīḥ Muslim*
3. *Sunan Abū Dāwūd*
4. *Sunan al-Tirmidhī*
5. *Sunan al-Nasā'ī*
6. *Sunan Ibn Mājah*

7. *Muwaṭṭa' Mālik*
8. *Musnad Aḥmad*
9. *Musnad al-Dārimī*

The Classification of Hadith

In the early generations, during the time of the Companions of the Prophet, it was quite easy to know the Sunnah of the Prophet ﷺ because the Companions had witnessed him directly. Unfortunately, in the generations that followed, some people would make false attributions to the Prophet ﷺ and claim that he said things which he had not said. They would do this with different intentions and agendas. This led to the scholars of Hadith putting an impressive amount of effort into preserving the Sunnah and distinguishing between authentic reports and false ones. They would study chains of narrations, the biographies of hadith narrators, and the texts of hadith in order to conclude which reports can comfortably be attributed to the Prophet ﷺ. Volumes have been written about those who narrated hadith so that we are able to know who the reliable and unreliable transmitters of hadith are. This effort was a collective one by many of the greatest scholars of Hadith, ensuring that the Sunnah of the Prophet ﷺ was preserved so that the Muslims may act upon it as Allah commanded them in the Qur'an.

This effort to study the Prophetic Traditions resulted in the formation of the science of Hadith. This became one of the most important of the Islamic sciences. It discusses chains of narration, different types of ahadith, the conditions for an authentic hadith, the different methods of transmitting hadith, the *fiqh* (understanding) of ahadith, and other relevant areas. Separate books have been authored in this science, known as *uṣūl al-ḥadīth* or *muṣṭalaḥ al-ḥadīth*, from the fourth century onwards. Some prominent works in this field include, *Maʿrifat ʿUlūm al-Ḥadīth* by Ḥākim al-Naysābūrī (d. 405 AH) and *Maʿrifat Anwāʿ ʿUlūm al-Ḥadīth* by Imam Abū ʿAmr ibn al-

Ṣalāḥ (d. 643 AH).

Studying the sciences of Hadith is an essential part of Islamic studies. We can only understand the Qur'an and the Shariah if we have a strong grounding in the sciences of Hadith and a good understanding of the *fiqh* of Hadith.

However, Hadith studies is usually a subject for the most dedicated of learners because it requires attention to detail. For instance, there are many classifications and categories of Hadith. Advanced readers can refer to the *Muqaddimah* by Ibn Ṣalāḥ which is also available in English. Readers who have access to Arabic can refer to many resources such as *al-Irshād* by al-Nawawī (which he later summarised in his *Taqrīb*), al-Suyūṭī's *Tadrīb al-Rāwī,* Ibn Kathīr's *Ikhtiṣār 'Ulūm al-Ḥadīth*, al-Zarkashī's *al-Nukat,* al-'Iraqi's *al-Taqyīd wa al-Īḍāḥ* and Ibn Ḥajar al-'Asqalānī's *Nukhbat al-Fikr*.

As a beginner, you should know that scholars have made four major classifications of hadith based on the soundness of the hadith in terms of the reliability and memory of its reporters:

1. *Ṣaḥīḥ* (rigorously authentic)
2. *Ḥasan* (good)
3. *Ḍa'īf* (weak)
4. *Mawḍū'* (fabricated)

Ṣaḥīḥ (rigorously authentic)

This is defined by Ibn Ṣalāḥ as a hadith which has a continuous chain of narrators (*isnād*), who have narrated the hadith from only trustworthy (*thiqah*) narrators (those with perfect memory and uprightness) and it (the hadith) is free from irregularities (in the text) and defects (in the *isnād*). Such as: Mālik—from Nāfi'—from 'Abdullāh ibn Umar.

Ḥasan (good)

Al-Tirmidhī defines *ḥasan* as a hadith which is not irregular (*shādh*) nor contains a disparaged reporter in its chain of narrators, and is reported through more than one channel. Examples of *ḥasan* ahadith are those which have been reported by: 'Amr ibn Shu'ayb—from his father—from his grandfather or Muḥammad ibn 'Amr—from Abū Salamah—from Abū Hurayrah.

_Ḍa'īf_ (weak)

A weak hadith is a hadith which has failed to meet the standard of *Ṣaḥīḥ* or *ḥasan*. It is usually one that has faults in the continuity of the chain of narrators (*isnād*) or has a fault in a narrator in terms of lack of reliability either in memory or uprightness.

Mawḍū' (fabricated)

These are ahadith which the Prophet Muhammad ﷺ never said, but due to personal motives, were fabricated and attributed to him. A fabricated hadith can be detected either because one of the narrators is known to be a liar or because the text is of an obnoxious nature, thus going against the principles of Islam. For example, it is (falsely) attributed to the Prophet Muhammad ﷺ that he said, 'A negro will fornicate when his belly is full and steal when he is hungry.' This is fabricated due to its obnoxious nature, hence going against the noble character of the Prophet Muhammad ﷺ.

Oftentimes though, the wordings of a fabricated hadith may be non-offensive or even sound sensible. For example, 'To return one *dāniq* (a sixth of a dirham) to its owner is better than worshipping (Allah) for seventy years.' At such instances, scrutinising the hadith based on the thoroughly developed science of hadith classification would help us determine if it was in fact narrated by the Prophet Muhammad ﷺ or simply made up and falsely attributed to him.

1

What Makes Allah Happy

اللَّهُ أَشَدُّ فَرَحًا بِتَوْبَةِ أَحَدِكُمْ مِنْ أَحَدِكُمْ بِضَالَّتِهِ إِذَا وَجَدَهَا

Abū Hurayrah ﷺ reported the Messenger of Allah ﷺ as saying: 'Allah is more pleased with the repentance of His servant when he turns regretfully towards Him than one of you would be on finding his lost camel.'

Imagine you are on a journey in a remote area such as the desert or jungle. You travel deep into the desert, cut off from all contact with other people. Your survival to reach your destination and out of the desert is your mode of transport, without which you are certain to perish. Unfortunately, your mode of transport is lost or broken. You face the prospect of certain death and so you try your best to find your mode of transport or fix the problem with it, but it is without success. After days, when the food and water supplies start depleting, the situation grows even more desperate and your hope of getting out of

One day, when the Prophet Muhammad ﷺ was walking somewhere, he came across a shopkeeper selling grain (or corn). The food had been presented in a pile to attract people to buy it, but it caught the attention of Prophet Muhammad ﷺ. He approached it and placed his hands on the foodstuff only to find that it was damp. Knowing that the grain should not be moist, the Prophet ﷺ asked the shopkeeper why it was damp. The shopkeeper told the Prophet Muhammad ﷺ that rainwater had fallen on it. The Prophet ﷺ told the man that his conduct failed to meet high standards and expectations, and that he had the responsibility to make this fault with the food apparent to his customers. He then warned the shopkeeper and told him that those who cheat are not members of the Muslim community.

The ethical and moral lessons from this hadith are great and immense, and in a day and age where we sell more things than ever before, this hadith is highly pertinent to our lives today. With apps and online services, we can sell almost any item, new or used. The temptation to sell a mobile phone, cars or any other merchandise which is faulty, while concealing those faults from the buyer is very real. The seller thinks that by doing this they have gained, and the merchandise becomes the problem of the buyer. This is, in fact, cheating and an act of dishonesty. What is ironic is that if the same person were to buy faulty goods themselves, they would feel upset and would expect to exchange them for proper goods or get a refund. The main problem with cheating is that it hurts feelings and damages trust, which leads to animosity between people, and animosity creates discord and disunity.

The Prophet ﷺ told Muslims that they cannot be considered to be a part of the Muslim community if they cheat. When selling something, it is our duty to point out all the faults to the buyer and let them decide if they want to buy it or not. Remember, even if the one who cheats is able to escape justice in this world, they will certainly not be able to escape it on the Day of Judgement. There will be reckoning for it and there will be justice established for the victim of cheating.

The Tricks of Dajjāl (Anti-Christ)

عن أبى سعيد الخدرى ﵁ قَالَ حَدَّثَنَا رَسُولُ اللَّهِ صلى الله عليه
وسلم يَوْمًا حَدِيثًا طَوِيلاً عَنِ الدَّجَّالِ فَكَانَ فِيمَا حَدَّثَنَا قَالَ يَأْتِي
وَهُوَ مُحَرَّمٌ عَلَيْهِ أَنْ يَدْخُلَ نِقَابَ الْمَدِينَةِ فَيَنْتَهِى إِلَى بَعْضِ السِّبَاخِ
الَّتِى تَلِى الْمَدِينَةَ فَيَخْرُجُ إِلَيْهِ يَوْمَئِذٍ رَجُلٌ هُوَ خَيْرُ النَّاسِ — أَوْ مِنْ
خَيْرِ النَّاسِ — فَيَقُولُ لَهُ أَشْهَدُ أَنَّكَ الدَّجَّالُ الَّذِى حَدَّثَنَا رَسُولُ
اللَّهِ صلى الله عليه وسلم حَدِيثَهُ فَيَقُولُ الدَّجَّالُ أَرَأَيْتُمْ إِنْ قَتَلْتُ
هَذَا ثُمَّ أَحْيَيْتُهُ أَتَشُكُّونَ فِى الأَمْرِ فَيَقُولُونَ لاَ — قَالَ فَيَقْتُلُهُ ثُمَّ
يُحْيِيهِ فَيَقُولُ حِينَ يُحْيِيهِ وَاللَّهِ مَا كُنْتُ فِيكَ قَطُّ أَشَدَّ بَصِيرَةً مِنِّى
الآنَ — قَالَ — فَيُرِيدُ الدَّجَّالُ أَنْ يَقْتُلَهُ فَلاَ يُسَلَّطُ عَلَيْهِ

Abū Sa'īd al-Khudrī ﵁ reported: 'The Messenger of Allah ﷺ one day gave a detailed account of the Dajjāl and in that it was also included: "He would come but would not be allowed to enter the mountain passes to Madinah. So he will alight at some of the barren tracts near Madinah, and a person who would be the best of men, or one from amongst the best of men, would say to him: 'I bear testimony to the fact that you are Dajjāl about whom Allah's Messenger ﷺ had informed us.' The Dajjāl would say: 'What is your opinion if I kill this person, then I bring him back to life; even then will you harbour doubt in this matter?' They would say: 'No.' Dajjāl would then kill him and then bring him back to life. When he would bring that person to life, that person would say: 'By Allah, I have not been more certain of the fact (that you are the Dajjāl) than at the present time.' The Dajjāl would then make an attempt to kill him but he would not be able to do that.'"

This world will end and there is no doubt about it. It is a fact that no one can deny whether they are a believer or a disbeliever. The Qur'an and the Prophet Muhammad ﷺ have told us in clear terms about the end of the world, and this is a fundamental part of the Islamic faith. No one knows when the world will end, but the Prophet ﷺ did tell us about some of the signs that indicate that the Final Hour is close. One of the major signs of the Final Hour is the emergence of the Dajjāl. The Dajjāl is the embodiment of evil and stands for everything ungodly. Allah will send him as a trial and tribulation upon humankind. Allah will endow Dajjāl with some special powers which the latter will use to fool people into believing he is God. Only strong believers and the faithful will not fall for his tricks.

Other ahadith suggest that the Dajjāl will appear at a time of famine and widespread hardship. The Dajjāl will come with a mountain of bread and a river of water; he will command the sky to bring rain; and the speed by which he will travel on earth will be like wind leaving behind condensation. He will claim that he is God, but he will be one-eyed and he will have the letters 'ك ف ر' (*ka-fa-ra,* the root letters of the word 'kāfir' which means 'disbeliever') on his forehead, and everyone, whether literate or illiterate, will be able to read it.

This hadith tells us that Dajjāl will be unable to enter Madinah, the city of the Prophet Muhammad ﷺ. In order to gain more support, Dajjāl will show off his one-off power of bringing back the dead to life.

When people will gather on the outskirts of Madinah to see what the commotion is about, a believing man will confront Dajjāl and tell him to his face that he is in fact the Dajjāl. In order to prove himself to be a god, Dajjāl will ask the people if they will believe in him if he kills someone and brings him back to life. The crowd will agree to this. Dajjāl will then proceed to kill the believing man. This killing is no illusion or trick we see on television; it will be a real act of killing. After that, Dajjāl, with the permission of Allah, will bring that man back to life. That man will then tell Dajjāl, with certainty, that he is the evil anti-Christ, and although Dajjāl will try to kill him again, he would not be able to do so.

The time when Dajjāl emerges will be an extremely tough time for the Muslims to hold onto their faith. The Prophet Muhammad ﷺ told us to seek refuge in Allah from the *fitnah* (trial and tribulations) of Dajjāl by saying: '*Allāhumma innī a'ūdhubika min fitnatil masīḥ al-dajjāl.*' Preparing for the end of times is the action of the wise, and so it would only be sensible to always make this prayer.

4

Signs of the Day of Judgement

قَالَ الْمُسْتَوْرِدُ الْقُرَشِيُّ عِنْدَ عَمْرِو بْنِ الْعَاصِ سَمِعْتُ رَسُولَ اللَّهِ
صلى الله عليه وسلم يَقُولُ تَقُومُ السَّاعَةُ وَالرُّومُ أَكْثَرُ النَّاسِ
فَقَالَ لَهُ عَمْرٌو أَبْصِرْ مَا تَقُولُ – قَالَ أَقُولُ مَا سَمِعْتُ مِنْ رَسُولِ
اللَّهِ صلى الله عليه وسلم قَالَ لَئِنْ قُلْتَ ذَلِكَ إِنَّ فِيهِمْ لَخِصَالاً
أَرْبَعًا إِنَّهُمْ لأَحْلَمُ النَّاسِ عِنْدَ فِتْنَةٍ وَأَسْرَعُهُمْ إِفَاقَةً بَعْدَ مُصِيبَةٍ
وَأَوْشَكُهُمْ كَرَّةً بَعْدَ فَرَّةٍ وَخَيْرُهُمْ لِمِسْكِينٍ وَيَتِيمٍ وَضَعِيفٍ
وَخَامِسَةٌ حَسَنَةٌ جَمِيلَةٌ وَأَمْنَعُهُمْ مِنْ ظُلْمِ الْمُلُوكِ

While Mustawrid al-Qurashī رضي الله عنه was with 'Amr ibn al-'Āṣ رضي الله عنه he reported to him, 'I heard Allah's Messenger ﷺ saying: "The Last Hour would come (when) the Romans would form a majority amongst people."' 'Amr said to him, 'Be sure of what you are saying.' He said, 'I say what I heard from the Messenger of Allah ﷺ.' Thereupon 'Amr ibn al-'Āṣ رضي الله عنه said, 'If you say that as a fact, then they

(Romans) have four qualities: They have the patience to undergo a trial; they immediately restore themselves to sanity after trouble; they attack again after flight; they (have the quality) of being good to the destitute, the orphans, and to the weak. And fifthly, the good quality in them is that they resist the oppression of kings.'

Why is it important for us to know the signs of the end of time? It is important for many reasons. We cannot do anything to prevent the events from taking place; they will happen without doubt. But if we know about the different signs of the end of time, then we can spot them and take even more measures to prepare for the end of the world.

This is an amazing hadith, something the Prophet Muhammad ﷺ told us over 1400 years ago. It is amazing because we are living in a time and age when we can witness this with our own eyes. Hadith commentators say that the word 'Romans' can mean Christians, the Caucasian race, or the geographical location in terms of what we now call the Western world or the Europeans and their global spread. We can see that the majority of the world's population are Christians, or Caucasians. When Mustawrid al-Qurashī made his comment, the great prophetic Companion 'Amr ibn al-'Āṣ ﷺ told him to be certain of his claim. Once reassured, 'Amr ibn al-'Āṣ ﷺ told him about some special characteristics of the so-called 'Romans'. These characteristics are very positive features which display the strength of the Romans as well as their moral conduct. The interesting thing to note here is that we can agree on these features and we can see them with our own eyes.

Let us have a look at the qualities. The first is that they have the patience to undergo a trial. If we look at Europe, we can see that they have this amazing ability to bounce back from any disaster, whether

6

Setting a Good Example

عَنْ أَبِي هُرَيْرَةَ أَنَّ رَسُولَ اللهِ صَلَّى اللهُ عَلَيْهِ وَسَلَّمَ قَالَ مَنْ دَعَا إِلَى هُدًى كَانَ لَهُ مِنَ الْأَجْرِ مِثْلُ أُجُورِ مَنْ تَبِعَهُ لَا يَنْقُصُ ذَلِكَ مِنْ أُجُورِهِمْ شَيْئًا وَمَنْ دَعَا إِلَى ضَلَالَةٍ كَانَ عَلَيْهِ مِنَ الْإِثْمِ مِثْلُ آثَامِ مَنْ تَبِعَهُ لَا يَنْقُصُ ذَلِكَ مِنْ آثَامِهِمْ شَيْئًا

Abū Hurayrah ﵁ reported that the Messenger of Allah ﷺ said: ‘He who called (people) to righteousness, there would be reward (assured) for him like the rewards of those who adhered to it, without their rewards being diminished in any respect. And he who called (people) to evil, he shall have to carry (the burden) of its sin, like those who committed it, without their sins being diminished in any respect.’

Doing good deeds is the best way to get close to Allah. Islam champions righteousness and encourages people to do as much good as they can. To excel in worship and get even closer to Allah, we shouldn't restrict ourselves to individual good deeds alone but also promote those good deeds and encourage others to do them as well. It is about setting a good example in society, which can be done at all levels.

Setting a good example at home can be, for example, fixing a day when the family will sit and learn some ahadith or memorise a part of the Qur'an together before having a family meal. Although this particular action was not done by the Prophet Muhammad ﷺ, because it is a good deed and no sin is involved, everyone will be rewarded. The person who started it off will be rewarded and he or she shall enjoy the extra rewards for telling others to do good.

At the mosque, for example, the imam can fix a particular day to teach the *tafsīr* of the Qur'an. At the work place, a day can be fixed to go out for a meal once a week or once a month to share thoughts on how to improve the locality or to learn something. Families in a vicinity can schedule a time every month to organise picking up litter and caring for the environment. The examples are endless and the opportunity to amass good deeds are limitless.

Like performing good deeds and encouraging others to do good deeds comes with great reward, committing bad deeds and encouraging others to do bad deeds comes with great sin and damnation. For example, if a person prepares a type of drug and consumes it then they are sinful, but if they also sell it to others and encourage others to consume it, then that person will suffer the consequences of the sins they have committed and will be burdened with the sins of all those who copied them. Both the leaders and the followers will suffer in committing sin but the person who started off the bad deed will be burdened with extra sin.

The lesson we can take from this hadith is that we should always stay away from setting a bad example in case others copy us, and instead we must always do good deeds and encourage others to do them too.

7

Beware of Backbiting

عَنْ أَبِي هُرَيْرَةَ أَنَّ رَسُولَ اللهِ صَلَّى اللهُ عَلَيْهِ وَسَلَّمَ قَالَ أَتَدْرُونَ مَا الْغِيبَةُ۞ قَالُوا اللهُ وَرَسُولُهُ أَعْلَمُ قَالَ ذِكْرُكَ أَخَاكَ بِمَا يَكْرَهُ قِيلَ أَفَرَأَيْتَ إِنْ كَانَ فِي أَخِي مَا أَقُولُ۞ قَالَ إِنْ كَانَ فِيهِ مَا تَقُولُ فَقَدِ اغْتَبْتَهُ وَإِنْ لَمْ يَكُنْ فِيهِ فَقَدْ بَهَتَّهُ

Abū Hurayrah ﵁ reported the Messenger of Allah ﷺ as saying: 'Do you know what is backbiting?' They (the Companions) said: 'Allah and His Messenger knows best.' Thereupon the Prophet ﷺ said: 'Backbiting is talking about your brother in a manner which he would not like.' It was said to him: 'What if what I say about my brother is true, then what is your opinion?' He said, 'If that thing is true then you have backbitten him, and if that is not then it is a slander.'

There can be no mistake about Islam's commitment to fostering love and brotherhood. Unity on account of faith is a pillar of social interaction in Islam, and it is so serious that Islam prohibits anything that will harm or affect social cohesion and brotherly love. Backbiting is one of the most common acts of sin people commit. Oftentimes, people do it without even realising it. It does not matter who you are, when you hear people talking ill of you it hurts and upsets you. In many cases, when people hear others talking ill of them, it turns into confrontation and arguments. It causes splits and breaks down friendships.

The seriousness of backbiting is mentioned in the Qur'an wherein Allah describes the act of backbiting through a horrific analogy. He says: *'O believers, avoid being excessively suspicious, for some suspicion is a sin. Do not spy, nor backbite one another. Would any of you like to eat the flesh of his dead brother? Surely you would detest it. Have fear of Allah. Indeed, Allah is the Accepter of repentance, Most Merciful'* (*al-Ḥujurāt* 49: 12). This verse is a clear message of the serious evil of backbiting. No other sin is equated to eating the flesh of another person. Allah asks the believers if they would like to eat the flesh of another person, because it is regarded as such a vile act that it will make many physically sick thinking about it. If that is the case, then backbiting must be regarded in the same light and should make us physically sick, impelling us to avoid it altogether.

Many of us may think that backbiting is when untrue things are being said about someone. However, through this hadith, the Prophet Muhammad ﷺ teaches us what backbiting really is. He explains that backbiting is anything we say about somebody, which if they were to hear, would hurt their feelings. Additionally, when one of the Companions asked the Prophet ﷺ what if the backbiting consisted of facts, he replied that even if it were true it was backbiting, but if what was said was false then the sin is greater, as that is considered slander.

Thus, all effort must be made to avoid talking ill about people

The most important identity we have is our name. It is such a special thing, because everyone in the world will know us by our names, and Allah on the Day of Judgement will call us by that name. In this hadith, the Prophet Muhammad ﷺ changed the name of a girl because it was not suitable. Imagine naming someone Horrible, Nasty, Naughty, or Disobedient. It is neither nice nor pleasant.

There are two major lessons we can learn from this hadith. Firstly, as parents, it is vital to give our children beautiful names; names which carry personality, history, and honour. Remember, it is a child's right that you give them a beautiful name. Once a man came with his son to Umar ibn al-Khaṭṭāb ﷺ and complained that his son does not listen to him. Umar ibn al-Khaṭṭāb ﷺ asked the boy a few questions to help him understand why the boy does not listen to his father. One of his questions enquired about his name. The boy replied, 'My name is Maḍrūb (the beaten one).' Umar ﷺ turned to the father and asked him what can he expect when he has failed to observe the rights of the child? How can he expect the child to be obedient to him?

The second lesson we can learn is that if someone was named improperly, it is praiseworthy to change their name to a better one. Naming children has a cultural element to it. In some cultures, parents name their children after birds and fruits. This should be avoided. The best names are the Names of Allah, the names of the Prophets, and the names of the Prophet's Companions. The most beloved name with Allah is either 'Abd al-Raḥmān or 'Abdullāh.

Knock Knock! Who's there?

عن أبي موسى الأشعرى قال قَالَ رَسُولُ اللهِ صَلَّى اللهُ عَلَيْهِ وَسَلَّمَ
إِذَا اسْتَأْذَنَ أَحَدُكُمْ ثَلَاثًا فَلَمْ يُؤْذَنْ لَهُ فَلْيَرْجِعْ

Abū Mūsā al-Ash'arī ⁓ reported that the Messenger of
Allah ⁓ said: 'When any one of you seeks permission
three times and he is not granted permission, he should
come back.'

Islam is not a religion which simply focuses on spiritual acts of
worship. It is a complete way of life and it deals with all aspects of
life—all the way from how to run a country, to how a person should
clip their nails. Social protocols, decorum, and etiquettes were much
emphasised by the Prophet Muhammad ⁓ because they help build
character and strengthen personalities. One of the social protocols
Islam wanted to highlight was the respect for personal space and
privacy. To this end, the Prophet Muhammad ⁓ taught us that we
must seek permission before we enter the house of another person. It

should be noted that the permission to enter a house is not restricted to dwellings only but rather any space a person occupies as personal space such as office space, working area, or restricted zones. The rule does not apply to public spaces such as shops, roads, and the like.

It does not matter who you are, you must seek permission. Once Abū Mūsā al-Ash'arī ﷺ was summoned by Umar ibn al-Khaṭṭāb ﷺ. Abū Mūsā ﷺ came to him and knocked on the door three times but did not get a response and so he left. When Umar ﷺ caught up with him he asked why he did not attend. Abū Mūsā ﷺ replied that he did and sought permission to enter but when he did not receive permission to enter, he returned.

Al-Nawawī, the great Hadith scholar and jurist, explains this hadith in detail. He said that seeking permission is a necessary requirement because the Qur'an demands it. It is a Sunnah to combine invoking greetings upon the people of the household and seeking permission to enter. The way to do this is to first greet people with the *salām* and then seek permission by asking, 'May I enter?' Some scholars like al-Māwardī said that if the host sees you then it is better to say the *salām* first and then seek permission, but if he or she does not see you then you should seek permission and then say the greetings of *salām* upon entering.

If a person seeks permission three times and does not receive a response, what should they do? Al-Nawawī says that if a person thinks that the host has not heard them then there are three opinions: first, the person should return; second, they may repeat the request to enter; third, if a person starts off with seeking permission, then they should return but if they start off with greetings, then they may ask again.

We should be mindful of personal space and privacy. It is not permissible for children to enter the bedrooms of their parents without their permission, and in like manner, parents should be mindful of knocking on the door of their children's rooms before they enter. The same applies to siblings. This behaviour fosters respect for all and creates a sense of consideration.

10

Private Chit-chat in Front of Others

عَنْ عَبْدِ اللهِ بن مسعود قَالَ قَالَ رَسُولُ اللهِ صَلَّى اللهُ عَلَيْهِ وَسَلَّمَ
إِذَا كُنْتُمْ ثَلَاثَةً فَلَا يَتَنَاجَى اثْنَانِ دُونَ صَاحِبِهِمَا فَإِنَّ ذَلِكَ يُحْزِنُه

'Abdullāh ibn Mas'ūd ﷺ reported the Messenger of Allah ﷺ as saying: 'If you are three, two should not converse secretly to the exclusion of your companion for that hurts his feelings.'

Embedded throughout the teachings of Islam is the concept of not causing harm to others. Our emotional wellbeing is equally important as our physical wellbeing. Allah has created human beings as delicate and fragile creatures who are highly emotional.

Being such emotional creatures, we can get upset by the slightest of issues. In this hadith, the Prophet Muhammad ﷺ wanted to teach his followers the etiquettes of social conduct and how to behave in a group. He told Muslims that whispering between two people should not take place in the presence of others. This is because it may cause suspicion and worry in the minds of those people that something is being said about them. The warning is severe if the situation consists of danger or uncertainty such as being stranded in a place or when in darkness or on a journey.

The same can be said if there are people of different languages and two of them speak a language unfamiliar to the other person. In such a situation, the two must refrain from speaking to each other in a language foreign to the third. However, if it is a large gathering then there is no problem in two people speaking privately or in another language because the worry of causing harm and upset is eliminated.

The major lesson we can learn from this hadith is that any cause of distress to another person is not acceptable in Islam and all efforts must be made to avoid it.

11

Meaning of Good Dreams and Bad Dreams

عَنْ أَبِى قَتَادَةَ عَنْ رَسُولِ اللهِ صَلَّى اللهُ عَلَيْهِ وَسَلَّمَ أَنَّهُ قَالَ الرُّؤْيَا
الصَّالِحَةُ مِنَ اللهِ ◉ وَالرُّؤْيَا السَّوْءُ مِنَ الشَّيْطَانِ فَمَنْ رَأَى رُؤْيَا
فَكَرِهَ مِنْهَا شَيْئًا فَلْيَنْفُثْ عَنْ يَسَارِهِ وَلْيَتَعَوَّذْ بِاللهِ مِنَ الشَّيْطَانِ
لَا تَضُرُّهُ وَلَا يُخْبِرْ بِهَا أَحَدًا فَإِنْ رَأَى رُؤْيَا حَسَنَةً فَلْيُبْشِرْ وَلَا
يُخْبِرْ إِلَّا مَنْ يُحِبُّ

Abū Qatādah رضي الله عنه reported the Messenger of Allah ﷺ as saying: 'The good visions are from Allah and the evil dreams are from the Satan. If one sees a dream which one does not like, he should spit on his left side and seek the refuge of Allah from Satan. The dream will not do him any harm, and he should not disclose it to anyone. And if one sees a good vision, he should feel pleased but should not disclose it to anyone but whom he loves.'

Blessed is Allah who has created sleep as a means of relaxation so that we may regain strength after fatigue. The finite nature of humans means that we become weak after hard work. To regain our strength, we need to consume food and water, and then rest.

Everyone has experienced tiredness after a hard day's work. There would be days when we work until we're exhausted and feel as though we cannot do anything. But after a good night's sleep we feel fully recharged. This is the beauty of sleep.

There are many enigmas to sleep which have baffled scientists who are still trying to wholly understand it. One such enigma is dreams. Why do we dream? We know from the Qur'an that some dreams carry a message, but the interpretation of the dream depends on the person seeing the dream.

We also know that all of the dreams of the Prophets of Allah are a form of revelation (*wahī*). Let's take the example of the Prophet Ibrāhīm ﷺ who saw himself in a dream, sacrificing his son, Ismāʿīl ﷺ for the sake of Allah. Prophet Ibrāhīm ﷺ knew that this was a command from Allah, so he related the dream to his son, Ismāʿīl ﷺ. Ismāʿīl ﷺ, also a Prophet, knew that this was a command from Allah, and so he told his father to obey the command of Allah. The famous Qur'anic story of Prophet Yūsuf ﷺ is also an excellent example to prove that some dreams can have a serious message.

For ordinary people, the experience of dreams differs according to who they are. Once Ibn Sīrīn was sitting with his students when a man came to him and told him that he saw himself reciting *Surah al-Ikhlāṣ* in a dream. Ibn Sīrīn said to the man crossly, 'Go and repent to Allah for your sins; you shall never have children.' A few moments later, another man came to Ibn Sīrīn and told him the same thing—that he saw himself in a dream reciting *Surah al-Ikhlāṣ*. This time Ibn Sīrīn smiled and told the man in a cheerful voice, 'You are blessed, you will have many children and all of them will be *ḥuffāẓ* of the Qur'an.' The students of Ibn Sīrīn were baffled and asked their teacher why he gave two different interpretations when the dreams were identical.

Ibn Sīrīn explained that the first man was a man of bad character. Consequently, his dream meant that he will not have children because *Surah al-Ikhlāṣ* mentions, 'He neither begot nor was He begotten' (*al-Ikhlāṣ* 112: 3). The second man was a good, pious man so his dream was in line with the virtues of *Surah al-Ikhlāṣ*.

It is a fact that everyone has dreams. These visions that we have can either be wonderful, scary, or just plain confusing. Some dreams, however, make us anxious and become a cause of worry for us when we wake up. So, what should a person do when they have bad dreams? In this hadith, the Prophet Muhammad ﷺ has told us exactly what to do in such cases.

He teaches that if we have a bad dream, a dream that projects horrible things and frightening scenes, then that is from Satan. We should dry-spit to our left side (some ahadith state that the spittle should be thrice) and say '*a'ūdhu billāhi min al-shayṭān al-rajīm*'.[2] The Prophet ﷺ told us that Satan just wants us to worry and he reassured us that dreams cannot harm us.

However, if we have a good dream, the Prophet Muhammad ﷺ told us that we can feel happy about it and share it if we wish to, but only with the people we love. The wisdom behind this instruction is so that we reduce the chances of envy and the evil eye being cast upon us. The same wisdom can be witnessed in the story of Prophet Yūsuf ﷺ as well, when his father, Ya'qūb ﷺ had advised him to refrain from relating his dream to his brothers lest they become jealous of him. It is the sincere well-wishers who would be naturally more inclined and genuine in sharing our joys with us.

2 Phrase which means 'I seek refuge in Allah from Satan the outcast.'

12

Voluntary Prayers at Home

عَنْ زَيْدِ بْنِ ثَابِتٍ قَالَ قال رَسُولُ اللهِ صَلَّى اللهُ عَلَيْهِ وَسَلَّمَ إِنَّ
خَيْرَ صَلَاةِ الْمَرْءِ فِي بَيْتِهِ إِلَّا الصَّلَاةَ الْمَكْتُوبَةَ

Zayd ibn Thābit ﷺ reported that the Messenger ﷺ said: 'Pray in your homes, for the prayer observed by a man in the house is better except an obligatory prayer.'

Prayer is one of the greatest ways of worshipping Allah and it is the fastest way to draw closer to Him. It is narrated that Prophet Muhammad ﷺ said that there is nothing more beloved to Allah and nothing that draws a person closer to Him than when a person prays their compulsory (*farḍ*) prayers. By offering the compulsory prayers, a person reaches a degree of closeness to Allah, but he or she can continue to draw closer to Him by offering the voluntary prayers as well.

In this hadith, the Prophet Muhammad ﷺ wanted to teach us that the best place for praying the voluntary prayers is our home. There are several reasons for this. Worshipping Allah in seclusion is better because it helps us focus on our sincerity and devotion. Prayer at home also helps us to engage other members of our household with voluntary prayer. It invites the mercy of Allah upon the house and gives life to it.

However, we must mention in the same breath that the five daily prayers (for men) are best prayed in congregation at a mosque rather than at home. If prayer was ordained to be strictly a private affair, then religion and virtue in society would be hidden and consequently, promoting good and forbidding evil would not have a visible existence in society. By praying in congregation, religion can be seen as an active part of life. It brings people closer and makes them care for each other.

This hadith also teaches us that voluntary actions are what really reflect a person's commitment to a cause. Consider this: When we do something because it is our job or because we have no other choice, we wouldn't necessarily receive a lot of admiration for our deed because it is something that is expected of us. But when we do something beyond the call of duty, then our efforts are recognised and appreciated. It shows that we are dedicated, invested, and diligent. We are willing to sacrifice our time and effort for something that is dear to us. Similarly, voluntary deeds make us draw closer to Allah and elevates us to a special relationship with Him. Allah loves such a person to the extent that whenever they ask Allah for help, Allah rushes to help them.[3]

---

3 Al-Bukhari, *Sahih al-Bukhari*, Hadith no. 6137

13

Zero Tolerance to Weapons

عَنْ أَبِي مُوسَى عَنِ النَّبِيِّ صلى الله عليه وسلم قَالَ مَنْ حَمَلَ
عَلَيْنَا السِّلاَحَ فَلَيْسَ مِنَّا

Abū Mūsā al-Ash'arī ﵁ reported that Allah's Messenger ﷺ said: 'He who took up arms against us is not of us.'

Islam teaches us that all Muslims are brothers and sisters, and encourages everyone to live amicably. However, where humans are involved, problems inevitably follow. This is a natural part of human life and is unavoidable. Hence, Islam has laid down rules on how we can solve problems if and when they do arise. The easiest way to settle disputes is by involving trustworthy arbitrators in the resolution process. In Islamic law, this is called *taḥkīm*. The other alternative is to take the matter to court and let the judge decide who is right and who is wrong. This is the way misunderstandings and problems are resolved. There is no room for violence towards fellow citizens due to a dispute. Sadly, in today's age, it has become a common occurrence in many parts of the world for people to draw out weapons at the slightest of disagreements. Physical fights or attacks against other people is simply not allowed in Islam; even threatening them with arms is unlawful to the extent that the angels curse a person for brandishing their weapons at another person,[4] even if it was for a joke, it is still not permissible because there are certain things which are not a matter of jest. The issue is severe because of the fact that things can rapidly escalate and what started off as a joke can easily turn into something catastrophic. Now, if pointing a weapon for fun is a serious offence, then how much more serious do you think assaulting another person with a weapon would be?

In this hadith, the Prophet ﷺ clearly condemned and disowned those who wield weapons at others from the Muslim community. That in itself is a grievous warning which highlights the enormity of the offence.

The prohibition underlying this hadith falls under the principle of causing harm or distress to another person, which is considered a grave sin in Islam. In fact, the cornerstone of social interaction is to avoid causing harm or distress to another person. Let us consider that the Prophet Muhammad ﷺ told people who have eaten raw garlic to avoid attending congregational prayers[5] because the strong odour will cause others harm. If causing harm by strong odours on account of eating something is offensive, then anything more severe is surely condemned. This hadith also teaches us that Muslims are expected to exhibit appropriate behaviour. It is not possible for us to attain closeness to Allah while we physically or psychologically hurt others—regardless of how much prayer, charity or voluntary acts of worship we do.

4 Muslim, *Sahih Muslim*, Hadith no. 2616

5 Muslim, *Sahih Muslim*, Hadith no. 2616

Three Deadly Sins

عن أَبِي بَكْرَةَ قَالَ كُنَّا عِنْدَ رَسُولِ اللَّهِ صلى الله عليه وسلم فَقَالَ
أَلاَ أُنَبِّئُكُمْ بِأَكْبَرِ الْكَبَائِرِ ثَلاَثًا الإِشْرَاكُ بِاللَّهِ وَعُقُوقُ الْوَالِدَيْنِ
وَشَهَادَةُ الزُّورِ أَوْ قَوْلُ الزُّورِ وَكَانَ رَسُولُ اللَّهِ صلى الله عليه وسلم
مُتَّكِئًا فَجَلَسَ فَمَازَالَ يُكَرِّرُهَا حَتَّى قُلْنَا لَيْتَهُ سَكَتَ

Abū Bakrah ﵁ said: ‘We were in the company of the Messenger of Allah ﷺ when he said: “Should I not inform you about the most grievous of the grave sins?” He repeated it three times, and then said: “Associating anyone with Allah, disobedience to parents, false testimony or false utterance.” The Prophet was reclining, then he sat up, and he repeated it so many times that we wished that he would stop.’

Striving to gain closeness to Allah must be the goal of every Muslim who wishes to enter Paradise. As such, the requirement for entering Paradise is obedience to Allah, which includes not only doing the things He has commanded us to do, but also staying away from the things He has warned us against. In this hadith, the Prophet Muhammad ﷺ informed us of three major acts of disobedience which will prevent a person from entering Paradise. These offences are so severe that Prophet Muhammad ﷺ continuously repeated his statement until the Companions grew worried and wanted him to stop. Let's take a look at these offences.

First on the list was *shirk. Shirk* means to associate anyone or any object in the worship of Allah. This can be done in many ways; the most obvious can be seen where people worship idols they created with their own hands from metal, wood, stone or any other material. However, there are subtle ways *shirk* can be committed as well, such as believing other objects or beings have the same power as Allah. All forms of *shirk* must be avoided because it goes against the most fundamental aspect of Islam, *tawhīd,* the belief in the Oneness of Allah. If He wishes, Allah may forgive every other sin a person has committed, but He has refused to forgive a person who commits *shirk* and does not repent to Him.

Disobedience to parents is second on the list. This is an interesting point to note, because it is second both in this list mentioned by the Prophet ﷺ and also in the one mentioned by Allah in the Qur'an: *'And Allah has commanded to worship none but He, and to be dutiful towards parents'* (*al-Isrā'* 17: 23). Mentioning it second after the concept of *tawhīd* signifies the high level of importance that being dutiful towards parents has in Islam. Being dutiful towards them means to care for them, not to raise our voice to them, not to talk back to them, and not to be rude to them. A person cannot enter paradise if they are disrespectful towards their parents.

Third on the list is false testimony and false statement. Any lie or untrue statement is a false statement. Islam does not tolerate falsehood;

in fact, it came to abolish falsehood and establish truth. Therefore, making a false claim, intentionally lying, or saying something untrue goes against the values Islam came to establish.

Equally sinful is providing a false testimony in a court or in front of people so as to support the false claims of another person. This is utterly wrong because it leads to injustice wherein the rightful due of one person is taken by another. Remember, a judge is duty-bound to pass judgement based on the evidence presented to him. So by making a false testimony, multiple people, primarily the victim and their family, are adversely affected. The person making the false statement shares in the sin of this dreadful deed, and is prevented from entering Paradise because of it.

15

Never Fall for the Same Trick Twice

عن أبى هريرة عن النبى صلى الله عليه وسلم قال لاَ يُلْدَغُ الْمُؤْمِنُ مِنْ جُحْرٍ وَاحِدٍ مَرَّتَيْنِ

Abū Hurayrah reported that the Messenger of Allah ﷺ said: 'The believer does not allow to be stung twice from the same hole.'

Islam came to perfect the character of a believer, to teach us values, ethics, and noble virtues. It is an inescapable reality that there will always be people who have chosen a different path in life; a path not of righteousness or good, but one of taking advantage of the vulnerable, the weak, the trustworthy, and the good nature of other people. Any one of us could become the victims of people of poor character, those who do not hesitate to exploit others to make a short-term gain for themselves. No one is immune from this.

In this hadith, the Prophet Muhammad ﷺ taught us that, as believers, we should be alert and not become targets of scams, tricks and cheats.

There is an interesting story behind this hadith: A man from Makkah came to fight against Muslims during the Battle of Badr. He encountered the Prophet Muhammad ﷺ and lost the fight, but then pleaded with the Prophet ﷺ to spare him. The Prophet ﷺ spared him as he promised he will never fight against Muslims ever again. During the following battle, the Battle of Uhud, the same man broke his promise and came to fight against the Muslims. Once again, the man encountered the Prophet Muhammad ﷺ, and again he lost the fight. He pleaded for his life, making the same false promise again. This time the Prophet Muhammad ﷺ said that the character of a Muslim is that he or she does not fall for the same trick twice.

In the modern world, the concept of scams has diversified and there is a dedicated community of evil people trying to cheat others with false statements in order to make a gain in some way. Even the wisest among us can fall prey to such trickery, and there is no guaranteed way of avoiding it from happening to anyone. We can all see it in different situations. For instance, when friends borrow money from us but do not have the intention to pay it back, whereas we lend them the money because we never expected them to cheat us in the first place. In such cases, although falling victim to cheats and scams may be unavoidable, falling for the same trick twice is most certainly avoidable. If we have been tricked once, we should learn from it and be cautious.

This hadith teaches us two important things. Firstly, anyone can become a victim of trickery and deceit. This does not mean that the victim is unintelligent, rather it is their good character that made them have faith in the other person. They wouldn't think of cheating anyone, so they subconsciously assume the same of others around them. Secondly, the hadith teaches us that we must always be alert and should constantly learn from our past experiences. This is what will make us stronger believers and help us get closer to Allah.

16

The Clear Sign of Faith

عَنْ أَبِي هُرَيْرَةَ قَالَ جَاءَ نَاسٌ مِنْ أَصْحَابِ النَّبِيِّ صلى الله عليه
وسلم فَسَأَلُوهُ إِنَّا نَجِدُ فِي أَنْفُسِنَا مَا يَتَعَاظَمُ أَحَدُنَا أَنْ يَتَكَلَّمَ بِهِ
قَالَ وَقَدْ وَجَدْتُمُوهُ قَالُوا نَعَمْ قَالَ ذَاكَ صَرِيحُ الإِيمَان

Abū Hurayrah ﷺ reported that some people from amongst the Companions of the Prophet ﷺ came to him and said: 'We find in ourselves that which we consider too grave to express.' The Prophet ﷺ said: 'Do you really find that?' They said: 'Yes.' Upon this he remarked: 'That is clear faith.'

Modesty and shyness are important aspects of faith. They are important because they are key to building noble characteristics in a person. Having a sense of shame and the fear of embarrassment are essential ingredients for self-dignity, honour, and respect. We, as humans, are weak creatures composed of a fragile demeanour, and we have to contend with many challenges in life. One of the daily challenges we are faced with is contending with Satan, the sworn enemy of humankind. Human frailty means that we make mistakes and sometimes these mistakes haunt us for a very long time. Satan has many tricks up his sleeves to misguide people, and if he cannot misguide us then he tries to cause us maximum distress and anguish.

One of the ways Satan does this is by making us think of past wrong deeds in the hope of trying to make us feel embarrassed. In like manner, creating evil thoughts in our minds is another trick of Satan, because people who have faith are stressed out due to bad thoughts. These thoughts are no ordinary thoughts, rather their nature is so awful that they can make us sick.

However, when we feel this way, it actually indicates a very praiseworthy quality; it indicates the beauty of our faith. This is because it is our faith that makes us feel repulsed at evil thoughts.

Once, a group of people came to the Prophet Muhammad ﷺ and told him that they have thoughts which are so profound they cannot talk about it. They did not tell the Prophet ﷺ what thoughts they had nor did the Prophet ﷺ want to know. Some scholars say that these thoughts are regarding aspects of faith, but the hadith is broad and it can include any type of bad thoughts. The Prophet ﷺ commended them for not talking about it and told them that their refusal to entertain these thoughts is a sign of the strength of their faith. The Prophet ﷺ asking them, 'Do you really find that?' was not to express doubt in what they were saying, but an expression of happiness in the fact that the fruit of their faith in Islam had manifested.

This hadith teaches us that it is unavoidable to have unwelcomed thoughts which are embarrassing or evil, or even both. The important thing to do is not to entertain them or speak about them but instead say, '*a'ūdhu billāhi min al-shayṭān al-rajīm*' (I seek refuge in Allah from Satan, the outcast) and free the mind of that thought.

17

Collective Worship

عَنْ أُمِّ عَطِيَّةَ قَالَتْ أَمَرَنَا رَسُولُ اللَّهِ صلى الله عليه وسلم أَنْ نُخْرِجَهُنَّ فِي الْفِطْرِ وَالأَضْحَى الْعَوَاتِقَ وَالْحُيَّضَ وَذَوَاتِ الْخُدُورِ فَأَمَّا الْحُيَّضُ فَيَعْتَزِلْنَ الصَّلاَةَ وَيَشْهَدْنَ الْخَيْرَ وَدَعْوَةَ الْمُسْلِمِينَ قُلْتُ يَا رَسُولَ اللَّهِ إِحْدَانَا لاَ يَكُونُ لَهَا جِلْبَابٌ قَالَ لِتُلْبِسْهَا أُخْتُهَا مِنْ جِلْبَابِهَا

Umm 'Aṭiyyah ﵂ reported: 'The Messenger of Allah ﷺ commanded us to bring out on Eid al-Fitr and Eid al-Adha young women, menstruating women and covered ladies. Menstruating women kept back from the prayer place, but participated in goodness and supplication of the Muslims. I said: "Messenger of Allah, one of us does not have an outer garment (to cover her face and body)." He said: "Let her sister cover her with her outer garment."'

Community spirit is crucial for a healthy society. It is important to make everyone feel that they are a member of the community, because this membership comes with the responsibility to look out for each other. It creates a sense of care, protection, friendship, loyalty and makes people feel that they are a part of a family. Every religion, society, culture or country has special days where they collectively celebrate an event or occasion.

In Islam, there are two special days of celebration where families come together, put aside work and spend the day in the company of each other. They prepare delicious food and make special drinks to share with friends and neighbours. The celebration of Eid starts with the *takbīr*, where Muslims—men, women, and children—gather and exalt the Name of Allah. Then the collective prayer of Eid takes place. This prayer is unique to the two Eid days and cannot be prayed at any other time. In the spirit of celebration and to make it a community event, Islam encourages everyone to attend the gathering and join together in the remembrance of Allah; after all, celebrations in Islam are about showing gratitude for the blessings of Allah.

What we take from this hadith is that women are valued members of the community and should be regarded in high esteem. Men and women, both, are active participants and both have a part to play within society. In this hadith the Prophet ﷺ is addressing a woman and advising her to encourage other women to attend the Eid prayer and celebrations. Even menstruating ladies, who would not perform the ritual prayer, should attend. The presence of women and their participation in the gathering was important and pertinent to the balance of the Muslim community.

Eid is a special occasion during which Muslims are encouraged to exalt the Name of Allah by reciting the *takbīr*[6]. People should recite the

---

6 Ibn Abi Shaybah, *Musannaf Ibn Abi Shaybah*, vol 2, pp. 165-168, Al-Shafi'i, Al-Umm, vol. 1, p. 241

takbīr while going to the place of prayer and continue to do so until they arrive there. The fact that the Prophet Muhammad ﷺ encouraged women to participate in such a celebration demonstrates that women should be involved in community affairs and may participate in all aspects of society in a manner that befits their nobility.

The hadith also alludes to the permissibility of women attending the prayer place in general, outside of the Eid days. Since the hadith mentions that menstruating women are allowed to attend the Eid congregation and are even encouraged to partake in the remembrance of Allah, while it commands her to keep away from the prayer place, we can infer that she is permitted to attend the congregational prayer too when she isn't in a state of menstruation. In fact, as we will see in Hadith 31 of this book, the Prophet Muhammad ﷺ has instructed men not to prevent the women of their household from going to the mosque, even though their houses are better places of prayer for them.[7] As such, Islamic organizations and mosques must make provision to cater to the needs of women attendees.

It is important to note that some scholars have discouraged women from attending prayer in congregation. They argue that times have changed and that during the time of the Prophet ﷺ, men and women behaved in a more sensible manner, observing decorum of gender segregation. But as time passed these values diminished and some worrying traits started to appear. This was noted by the Prophet's wife, 'Ā'ishah ؓ who remarked that had the Prophet ﷺ been alive then and seen what was happening, then he too would have prohibited women from attending collective prayer.[8]

While this opinion does exist among scholars it is important to keep in mind that, despite being based on authentic sources, scholars'

7 Abu Dawud, *Sunan Abi Dawud*, Hadith no. 567

8 Al-Bukhari, *Sahih al-Bukhari*, Hadith no. 869, Muslim, *Sahih Muslim*, Hadith no. 445

person drinks, they lose the ability to control themselves and, more importantly, what they say and how they behave. They rave like lunatics and people mock and laugh at them. While they are under the influence of alcohol, they lose all form of respect and honour and reduce themselves to a fool or a joke in the eyes of people. This loss of dignity was on account of something that was voluntarily consumed. This is the minor aspect of the harm of alcohol. In current times, we can see the devastating effects alcohol has on society, families and national services such as the police and health services, and much more. Intoxicants break societies and families and the people who suffer the most are the poor.

When prohibiting alcohol, the Qur'an talks specifically about wine, so the Prophet Muhammad ﷺ wanted to clarify the rule in Islam regarding all forms of intoxicants. The rule he mentioned to guide us is that if any consumable leads to intoxication, then it becomes unlawful and Muslims are not allowed to consume it. Eating things which harm the mind, body and soul are prohibited in Islam because it goes against the Islamic principle of preserving these things.

Any substance which has the harmful effects of addiction and intoxication is outlawed in Islam. What makes this hadith so interesting is that we can see, in our times more than any other time in history, the harmful effects of all types of intoxication. This is because in current times, man has created so many different types of drugs for the sake of getting a 'high'.

The negative consequence of consuming alcohol is felt not only in this world but will also be carried on to the Hereafter. The Prophet ﷺ has told us that a person who consumes intoxicants, becomes addicted to it, and does not repent will not get to drink from the river in Paradise.[9]

9 Muslim, *Sahih Muslim*, Hadith no. 4963

19

Torture is Unlawful in Islam

عَنْ هِشَامِ بْنِ حَكِيمِ بْنِ حِزَامٍ أنه مَرَّ بِالشَّامِ عَلَى أُنَاسٍ وَقَدْ أُقِيمُوا فِي الشَّمْسِ وَصُبَّ عَلَى رُءُوسِهِمُ الزَّيْتُ فَقَالَ مَا هَذَا قِيلَ يُعَذَّبُونَ فِي الْخَرَاجِ فَقَالَ أَمَا إِنِّي سَمِعْتُ رَسُولَ اللَّهِ صلى الله عليه وسلم يَقُولُ إِنَّ اللَّهَ يُعَذِّبُ الَّذِينَ يُعَذِّبُونَ فِي الدُّنْيَا

Hishām ibn Ḥakīm ibn Ḥizām ﵁ passed by some people in Syria who had been made to stand in the sun while olive oil was being poured upon their heads. He said: 'What is this?' It was said to him: 'They are being punished for (not paying) the *kharaj* (the government tax revenue on land).' Thereupon he said: 'I heard the Messenger of Allah ﷺ saying: "Allah will punish those who torture people in this world."'

The Prophet Muhammad ﷺ told us that Allah has written compassion for everything and therefore we must show compassion to every living creature—even if it is the animal we intend to slaughter for food; we are still not allowed to abuse that animal, rather we have to show it care and be mindful of its welfare. If there is a need to kill an animal such as a lion or a snake because it is endangering or will endanger the lives of other people, then that killing must be done with compassion and justice, without inflicting any more harm than needed. In another hadith, the Prophet Muhammad ﷺ told us how a woman had been condemned to Hell because she tortured a cat to death by starvation. This act of cruelty meant that she will answer for her crime in front of Allah and Allah will punish her for it.

No one has the right to mistreat another person to get their way. If people have behaved in a way that makes them deserve punishment, regardless of how bad their crime is, it does not give us the right to mistreat them. They should receive their punishment, firstly, from the authorities, not lay people; and even then, in a just way, not in a torturous manner.

This hadith shows how some rulers in the past thought that it was their right to deal with difficult or rebellious people by using force. The rulers did this because they had the power to do so. However, a more just punishment would have been, say, imprisoning the defaulters or even commanding that their property be seized, but they had no right to torment people regardless of the crime they had committed.

Rulers or members of the public who think they can torture people to make them confess or force them to do something should take heed of this warning from the Prophet Muhammad ﷺ that Allah will punish them; and the punishment of Allah is most severe. Inhumane ways of punishing people have no place in Islam. Unfortunately, the police and secret services in many countries believe that they have the right to abuse people in the name of upholding law and order. They might have the best interest of society in mind but it still does not justify maltreatment. A forced confession cannot be justice. The prosecution and conviction of people must be based on evidence and not something that is forced out of them by persecution.

This hadith also gives the general message that any act of cruelty is offensive. Even bullying someone will not go unaccounted for in front of Allah on the Day of Judgement. Sadly, bullying at schools and universities has become part of student life. 'Daring' someone to do something they don't want to is a just fancy word for forcing them; targeting someone and turning others against them is unjust boycotting; and 'playing pranks' on others could very well be torture. Peer pressure can do a lot of damage if we're not careful. It would help to periodically recall this hadith and check ourselves to see that we aren't physically or psychologically torturing anyone.

20

What Animals are Unlawful to Eat?

عَنِ ابْنِ عَبَّاسٍ قَالَ نَهَى رَسُولُ اللَّهِ صلى الله عليه وسلم عَنْ كُلِّ
ذِى نَابٍ مِنَ السِّبَاعِ وَعَنْ كُلِّ ذِى مِخْلَبٍ مِنَ الطَّيْرِ

Ibn 'Abbās ﷺ reported that the Messenger of Allah ﷺ prohibited the eating of all fanged beasts of prey, and all birds with talons.

Islam is a religion that promotes the welfare of people. The rules of Islam are centred on the principle of promoting physical and mental wellbeing in people. This concept is known as *ḥifẓ al-'aql* and *ḥifẓ al-nafs* in Arabic. Human beings are weak, and their weakness can be seen when there is a slight imbalance in the regular order of things. For example, if someone's blood pressure is too high or too low then that can cause major problems for them. Similarly, imbalances in your sugar levels, oxygen levels and many other similar examples all show how a slight change can be a cause of major problems. Mental health is equally vulnerable and a slight imbalance can upset the normal order of life. In summary, it is important to keep healthy, both physically and mentally. Physical wellbeing can be achieved by exercise, a healthy diet, and good sleep patterns, among other things; whereas mental wellbeing can be achieved by engaging in the *dhikr* (remembrance) of Allah, good companionship, positive thinking, and having a sense of dependence on Allah.

A common element in both physical and mental wellbeing, as contemporary studies suggest, is what we eat. Perhaps this is one of the reasons why Allah has commanded the Prophets and the believers to eat only that which is pure and good. A person on a balanced diet always feels good about themselves and has a positive outlook in life.

The rules in Islam regarding food are aimed at teaching humankind the best food to eat and that not everything that is edible should be eaten by people. Islam has allowed us, as Muslims, to eat meat and has called it good and pure. However, it does not mean that all types of meat are lawful. We are not allowed to eat the flesh of any carnivorous animal. The nature of these animals in comparison to herbivorous animals, most of which we are allowed to eat, is completely different and cannot be compared. Herbivores do not have vicious or ferocious characteristics while carnivores by their nature want to hunt and kill other animals. Such animals are not considered to be 'pure'. There isn't a legal rationale why Allah has made these animal unsuitable for Muslim consumption. A possible explanation may be because of the nature of what they eat and how they eat it. That is to say, carnivorous animals are dangerous animals, violent and vicious in their natural disposition. These attributes are not what a Muslim should have, rather, it is the opposite. Muslims should be kind, compassionate and gentle. Eating the flesh of such animals might have an adverse meta-spiritual effect on us without us realising it. We know that what we eat has a consequence on us physically and spiritually. Let's take drugs and alcohol. It is known that they have harmful effects on the body and the mind. It is due to the harmful nature of drugs and alcohol that it is prohibited for Muslims. Hence, Islam promotes wholesomeness and Allah wants to direct Muslims to having a wholesome life.

From a spiritual perspective when a person pollutes their body with unlawful foodstuff it spiritually pollutes their minds and souls. As a consequence of this, Allah rejects the supplications (*dua'*) of person who eats haram. This is why it is very important to eat pure and good food.

This hadith teaches us about halal food for Muslims. It plainly lays down the principle of what is considered lawful meat and what is not, i.e., all carnivorous animals and birds of prey are unlawful for Muslims to eat.

Seven Things to do and Seven Things not to do

على البراء بن عازب فسمعته يقول أمرنا رسول الله صلى الله
عليه وسلم بسبع ونهانا عن سبع أمرنا بعيادة المريض واتباع
الجنازة وتشميت العاطس وإبرار القسم أو المقسم ونصر
المظلوم وإجابة الداعى وإفشاء السلام ونهانا عن خواتيم أو عن
تختم بالذهب وعن شرب بالفضة وعن المياثر وعن القسى وعن
لبس الحرير والإستبرق والديباج

Barā'ibn 'Āzib ﷺ said: 'The Messenger of Allah ﷺ forbade us from doing seven (things) and commanded us to do seven (things). He commanded us to visit the sick, to follow the funeral procession, to answer the one who sneezes, to fulfil the vow, to help the poor, to accept invitations and to spread greetings. He forbade us to wear gold rings, to drink in silver (vessels), and to use the saddle cloth made of red silk, and to wear garments made of *qassī* (a type of clothing made from silk) material, or garments made of silk or brocade and velvet.'

There is no part of our lives which is free of rules. There is always a list of dos and don'ts that everyone must observe. Why, even a simple game made up at home for entertainment has a list of rules, because without rules even that simple game makes no sense. Therefore, in order for human life to be purposeful, there must be rules to help identify which actions are pleasing to our Creator and which are not.

With every prohibition, there is an element of temptation which allures a person to do it. It is regarded worship when a person is able to resist this temptation and avoid doing the deed. Acts of worship, on the other hand, are there to promote goodness, morals, and ethics. It is aimed at creating a conscious being who is careful not to harm anyone and instead cares for everyone.

This hadith lists seven things that Muslims are commanded to do and seven things they are forbidden to do by the Prophet Muhammad ﷺ. The seven commandments all relate to regular interaction with other people. What makes these commandments significant is that if they are not observed, it can cause disappointment and hard feelings.

For example, when a person is sick, they feel comforted by the company of people visiting them. It brings them solace because they know that there are people who care for them. If close family and friends do not visit, then it causes the ill person to be upset.

Observing the other items on the list in the same light, we will find that not greeting someone, or not accepting invitations, or not helping a person who is being oppressed, can cause serious ill feelings. This is why some of these actions are described in other ahadith as being from the rights of one Muslim over another. They are therefore not merely commendable acts, rather are duties upon us. When these practices become common in society, it leads to a well-bonded stable community in which people thrive, support and care for one another.

The easiest and most common of these actions is greeting someone. It is reported in another hadith that the Prophet Muhammad ﷺ said: 'You shall not enter Paradise until you believe; and you shall not believe until you love one another. Should I not tell you of something which will lead you to love one another? Spread *salām* (greetings) amongst one another'.[10]

There are seven things that are prohibited in this hadith; most are particular to men and one applies to both genders. Drinking in silver utensils is the one thing that is not allowed for men and women, while the rest of the prohibited articles apply to men only and are permitted for women.

A beautiful appearance is encouraged in Islam. The Prophet ﷺ said, 'Allah is beautiful, and He loves beauty'.[11] However, there are some restrictions to this, such as men being prohibited from wearing gold or pure silk. The hadith in discussion specifically mentions the prohibition of men wearing gold rings, but in another hadith the Prophet ﷺ said regarding gold and silk in general, 'These two are prohibited for men, but permissible for women.'[12] There are some interesting explanations for why gender played a role in prohibiting certain fashion items. Some scholars say that since beautification and jewellery are generally for women, men are encouraged to minimise it, and to avoid things which are seen to be feminine.

These prohibitions are of course, different to being smartly dressed and having a good appearance, which are certainly encouraged. Limited

---

10 Muslim, *Sahih Muslim*, Hadith no. 74

11 Muslim, *Sahih Muslim,* Hadith no. 1659

12 Abu Dawud, *Sunan Abi Dawud*, Hadith no. 4057

amounts of jewellery are also permitted for men, such as a watch or ring—as long as they are not made out of gold—as well as clothes which contain small amounts of silk, as this was explicitly allowed by the Prophet ﷺ in another hadith.[13]

Arrogance and showing off is another reason why these articles are forbidden for men. Islam considers arrogance to be a grave sin which Allah finds abominable. Since gold and silk are fashion items which are considered to be a mark of wealth and since men are more prone to be boastful of their wealth, the Prophet Muhammad ﷺ has forbidden his male followers from wearing them, lest it leads to pride and arrogance.

13 Muslim, *Sahih Muslim,* Hadith no. 1644

22

Criticising Food

عن أبي هريرة قال ما عاب رسول الله صلى الله عليه وسلم
طعاما قط كان إذا اشتهى شيئا أكله وإن كرهه تركه

Abū Hurayrah ﵁ reported that Allah's Messenger ﷺ never found fault with food (served to him). If he liked anything, he ate it and if he did not like it, he left it.

The blessings that Allah has showered upon us are countless. Allah says in the Qur'an: *'If you were to count the favours of Allah, you would not (be able to) enumerate them'* (*al-Naḥl* 16: 18). Think about the blessings of sight and hearing; how wonderful is it to see the sky, the colour of fruits, to listen to birds singing? And now imagine this blessing being taken away from you. How difficult would life be? How sad would that make you feel? Everything we have is a blessing from Allah and this hadith teaches us to be grateful for all the blessings we have.

Food is one of the greatest blessings. There is nothing better than a tasty plate of food, and no other creation of Allah has been honoured with food like human beings. However, at times, it feels like it is one of the most belittled blessings. When someone is used to eating whenever they like, it can be easy to forget how great a blessing even small amounts of food are.

This hadith provides some important teachings and guidance related to the etiquettes of eating and drinking. The etiquette described in this hadith is related to gratitude. The Prophet ﷺ never complained or made faces when food was served. If he liked it, he would eat it, and if he did not like it, he would simply leave it. There are three possibilities as to why food would not be to a person's liking. It can be that the person has a picky palate and doesn't like certain types of vegetables, certain cuts of meat, or certain types of seafood, and the like. Another reason could be that the ingredients were incorrect, and yet another reason that the cooking was faulty.

Whatever the reason is for the food to be disliked, complaining about it is a sign of ungratefulness. One of the expressions of the balanced and moderate life the Prophet ﷺ had is that he did not force himself to go against his comfort zone and eat things which he did not like. This shows that overeating or eating things which a person dislikes, only because food has been served, is not correct piety. However, disliking some food never led him to making ungrateful comments. He was polite and never became angry because of the food. If he did not like it, he did not eat it, but he did not complain.

The other side of this balanced approach is that leaving food that one likes is not necessarily a sign of piety either. The Prophetic teachings dictate that a Muslim should not overeat, even when food that he or she likes is served. Allah tells us in the Qur'an: *'Eat and drink, but do not be wasteful'* (*al-A'rāf* 7: 31). It is not a problem to eat any of the foods we enjoy, but we should remember to be grateful and eat in balanced amounts.

It is worth noting that this hadith may not apply to the modern day 'food critic'. This is because in the modern world, cooking is a professional industry and chefs claim to be experts. So, food critics do not criticise the food but in actuality they critique the chef's professionalism and claim to expertise.

23

Returning Lost and Found Property

عن زيد بن خالد الجهنى أنه قال جاء رجل إلى النبى صلى الله عليه وسلم فسأله عن اللقطة فقال اعرف عفاصها ووكاءها ثم عرفها سنة فإن جاء صاحبها وإلا فشأنك به

Zayd ibn Khālid al-Juhanī ﵁ reported that a man came to the Messenger of Allah ﷺ and asked him about picking up lost property. The Prophet said: 'Recognise it well, its bag and the strap (by which it is tied) then make announcement of that for a year. If its owner comes (within this time, return it to him), otherwise it is yours.'

Possessing property is important for human beings, because property means money, and money is a crucial means of survival in this world. As humans, it is commonplace for us to lose our possessions and when that happens, it can be very sad and upsetting. While acquiring any asset requires a lot of hard work, losing it, on the other hand, takes only seconds of neglect.

One of the aims of Islamic law is to preserve wealth. The property that people own is given a high level of sanctity and importance, because ensuring that each person's wealth is preserved is part of upholding justice and honouring humankind. Hence, Islam prohibits theft, deception, taking that which does not belong to us, and even the mishandling of lost-and-found property.

Once a man came to the Prophet Muhammad ﷺ and told him that he had found lost property and asked him what he should do with it. The Prophet ﷺ taught him that if a person finds something of value, they are not permitted to take ownership of it until after searching for its rightful owner. In this hadith, the Prophet Muhammad ﷺ placed a specific timeframe of one year on items which we find.

The person who found the property should pursue all reasonable means to find the rightful owner, such as writing a notice with a contact number and putting it up in the place it was found; handing it over to the police; or other similar measures to help find the owner. This does not mean that one must actively search for the owner every day for a whole year, but it implies to do what is practically sufficient in order to return the item to its owner. After this period passes, it is then permissible for the finder to use what they have found for their own benefit, whether that be money which they can spend or items which they can benefit from for their own use. However, they still will not have complete ownership, because if the rightful owner appears, it must be returned to the owner, as the Prophet Muhammad ﷺ explained. If the property has been used and is no longer available then the finder must give the owner its value in money or buy the same item for them.

These rulings apply to those items which are of significant value, and not to things of little value, because that would be a cause of hardship for people. For example, it would be unreasonable to require someone to search for the owner of a packet of sweets for a whole year.

Islam has therefore allowed one to take items of small value without searching for the owner if they are unknown. This is proven by the statement of the Prophet ﷺ when he found a date and said, 'If I did not fear this (date) may be charity, I would have eaten it.'[14] This shows that something which is of little value can be taken immediately without needing to search for the owner.

What constitutes 'value' is not something specified with exactness, but it is that which the average person considers valuable, according to the general custom of that time and place. Granted the value would then differ from person to person and place to place, one should still make sure to be reasonable to the best of their ability. If a person, for example, finds a £5 note on the street, they are allowed to take it and benefit from it, because the average person would not view this as something of great value, even if some individuals may. However, if someone found a wallet containing £100, then they should not take it until they have done their best to find the rightful owner; and if after a year, the owner has still not turned up, the finder may use the money for their own benefit.

14 Bukhari and Muslim, quoted via: *Riyad al-Salihin*, Hadith no. 588

24

Only Allah's Name Should be Taken for an Oath

عن عبد الله بن عمر عن رسول الله صلى الله عليه وسلم أنه أدرك عمر بن الخطاب في ركب وعمر يحلف بأبيه فناداهم رسول الله صلى الله عليه وسلم ألا إن الله عز وجل ينهاكم أن تحلفوا بآبائكم فمن كان حالفا فليحلف بالله أو ليصمت

'Abdullāh ibn Umar ﷺ reported that the Messenger of Allah ﷺ found Umar ibn al-Khaṭṭāb amongst some riders and he was taking an oath by his father. Allah's Messenger ﷺ thereupon said: 'Allah, the Exalted and Majestic, has forbidden you to take an oath by your fathers. He who takes an oath, must take it by Allah or keep quiet.'

Islam teaches us to be careful with the words we use, whether it be for the sake of being respectful towards other people or for the sake of being conscious of our obligatory belief towards Allah, His Messengers, and Islam. What we say has a profound impact on us as well as on those around us. We can say things which are extremely good or things which are extremely bad.

Once the Prophet Muhammad ﷺ told Muʿādh ؓ that people will be dragged to Hell because of what they say.[15] Guarding the tongue from falsehood is essential to building a strong relationship with Allah. A person cannot possibly expect to be close to Allah while they engage in false, useless or filthy talk.

At times in life, the things we say or the claims we make need to be strengthened so people know that we are serious. The strength of the statement is usually given by mentioning something that means the most to someone. It was a norm amongst the Arabs to swear by their parents or something of great value to them, if they wanted to give importance to a matter. This is still something that people often do today. Terms such as 'I swear by my mother's life' and 'I swear by my father's grave' are common in many countries across the world. Islam, however, has forbidden this practice.

This hadith recounts the time when the Prophet Muhammad ﷺ came across Umar ibn al-Khaṭṭāb ؓ as he was taking an oath on his father's name. The Prophet ﷺ stopped and prohibited him from doing so and told him that swearing by anything other than Allah is unlawful.

Although this hadith mentions taking an oath by parents' names, its prohibition is, nevertheless, universal and using any other person or object to swear by is considered to be a sin. It is prohibited because one only takes an oath and swears by those things which are sacred and important to them. Islam came to fill our hearts with a glorification of Allah more than anything else. When people take oaths by their parents more seriously than their oaths by Allah, there is an indication that the reverence and glorification of Allah is deficient. This is what led some scholars to describing such an action as being a form of *shirk*, because

15 Al-Tirmidhi, *Sunan al-Tirmidhi,* Hadith no. 2619

one has essentially equated something else to Allah in veneration.

In the Qur'an, Allah swears by many different things, such as the sun, the moon, the stars, the skies, and so on. This is repeated in the Qur'an to remind us of the greatness of the creation of Allah, which in turn reminds us of the greatness of the One who created these things. However, this is something that is exclusive to Allah, who swears by whatever He wills. Human beings, on the other hand, are taught to limit taking oaths by Allah's Name only.

25

Bequests Cannot be More Than One-third

عن سعد بن أبى وقاص قال عادنى رسول الله صلى الله عليه وسلم فى حجة الوداع من وجع أشفيت منه على الموت فقلت يا رسول الله بلغنى ما ترى من الوجع وأنا ذو مال ولا يرثنى إلا ابنة لى واحدة أفأتصدق بثلثى مالى؟ قال لا؟ قلت أفأتصدق بشطره؟ قال لا الثلث والثلث كثير إنك أن تذر ورثتك أغنياء خير من أن تذرهم عالة يتكففون الناس ولست تنفق نفقة تبتغى بها وجه الله إلا أجرت بها حتى اللقمة تجعلها فى فى امرأتك

Saʿd ibn Abī Waqqāṣ ﵁ said: 'The Messenger of Allah ﷺ visited me in my illness which brought me near death in the year of the Farewell Pilgrimage. I said: "O Messenger of Allah, you can well see the pain with which I am afflicted, and I am a man possessing wealth, and there is none to inherit me except one daughter. Should I donate two-thirds of my property?" He said: "No." I said: "Should I give half of my property as a donation (*Ṣadaqah*)?" He said: "No." He then said: "Give a third (in charity) and even that is a lot. To leave your heirs rich is better than to leave them poor, begging from people. You would never spend anything seeking the pleasure of Allah, except that you will be rewarded for it, even for a morsel of food that you put in your wife's mouth."'

Every parent strives to give the best to their children when they are alive. They work hard to provide food, clothing, shelter and education for them, and try to fulfil all their needs and wishes in life. Providing children with financial help when they are older is also important and sometimes needed. This need of the child does not end once the parent's life is over. So, it is important for parents to make an effort to leave something for their children after their death.

Once when Sa'd ibn Abī Waqqāṣ ﷺ was ill and feared that he may pass away, he consulted the Prophet Muhammad ﷺ when he paid him a visit, about donating a portion of his wealth in charity. Although he was prepared to donate a large portion of his wealth, the Prophet ﷺ told him to be balanced in using his wealth and to put those under his responsibility first. The Prophet ﷺ said, 'Begin with those under your care.' While the Prophet ﷺ allowed him to donate some of his wealth as a will, he limited the portion to a third. This means that no more than a third of one's wealth can be written in a will. The responsibility to ensure that a person's children and those under his responsibility have something to help themselves with is a priority, particularly if they are vulnerable and do not have other sources of sufficient income. The

Prophet ﷺ explained to Sa'd ؓ that it is better for him to leave his children and other inheritors rich and content, as opposed to leaving them to struggle and seek help from others.

This hadith instructs that a person cannot give more than one-third of their estate away and by extension, they may not bequeath anything to their heirs as they will automatically inherit from them and their portion is fixed by the Qur'an. The Prophet ﷺ further emphasised the importance of prioritising those that come under a person's responsibility.

He explained to Sa'd ؓ that even feeding one's own wife counts as an act of goodness and charity. Therefore, one should not think that charity and good deeds is only in giving to non-family members. In fact, helping needy family members is a greater act of good than helping others, because this means that one is not only helping those in need, but also keeping good relations with relatives. Although leaving behind a will is a noble action, it is not something compulsory. If a person felt that they will leave behind needy inheritors and thus leave all their wealth for them, as opposed to giving a portion of it away to others or other good causes, then he may do so.

This hadith teaches Muslims a number of things. It teaches us that we have a right to bequeath and make a will. We have the freedom to give away up to one-third of our estate to whomever or whatever cause we like. The hadith also shows us that every good thing a person does for the sake of Allah is counted as a charity. Finally, this hadith also teaches us that it is prohibited to give in excessive charity. Because donating most of our wealth and leaving a little behind for our family will cause them harm in the long term, such a practice is disallowed in Islam.

Taking Back a Gift

عن ابن عباس عن رسول الله صلى الله عليه وسلم قال العائد
فى هبته كالكلب يقىء ثم يعود فى قيئه

Ibn 'Abbās ﷦ reported that the Messenger of Allah ﷺ
said: 'The one who takes back his gift is like the dog that
throws up and then swallows it back.'

Exchanging gifts is one of the best ways to bring hearts closer and
to strengthen relationships, particularly between family members.
Gift-giving is an international and global culture practised by every
person. Gifts are given mostly at times of celebrations such as weddings,
the birth of a child and the like. In some cultures, gift-giving is a very
formal occasion and a lot of thought, planning and expense goes into
it. Since gifts can have a strong impact on people and the way we feel
towards one another, Islam has taught us some etiquettes related to
gift-giving.

The first is that one should accept gifts from others. The Prophet Muhammad ﷺ would not accept donations and charity for himself, but he would always accept gifts.[16] Refusing to accept gifts offered by others has a clear potential to cause ill feelings, and the one who has their gift rejected can easily feel offended.

Another important etiquette which relates to gifts is that one should not change their mind on gifting someone after they have made the intention to do so; and if a person has promised to give something to someone then they must definitely fulfil that promise of a gift. There are several reasons for this. The first is that we are always discouraged from changing our minds about noble actions. If someone intends to give to charity or fast, or to perform any good deed, then they should not allow the whispers of Satan to put them off completing what they intended to do. Any excuses which may seem to be valid to justify changing our minds about noble actions should be brushed aside and ignored. Of course, in situations of potential harm, it may be necessary to change our mind. For instance, one may intend to give a monetary gift to a friend, but then realise that they do not have enough money to pay the month's rent. In this case, they must prioritise themselves and those they are responsible for before they perform additional good deeds. However, this is an exception to the general rule that this hadith addresses.

Secondly, gifting or promising to gift something to someone, only to then change your mind, could cause offense to people. It may even occur to them that you no longer see them as worthy of receiving a gift, which is what caused you to change your mind. On top of this, it is seen to be a lowly act of conduct to go back on a gift that you gave or promised to give. In order to avoid these harmful consequences, the Prophet Muhammad ﷺ disallowed a person from going back on gifts. This understanding is not limited to just physical gifts, rather it also

16 Al-Bukhari, *Sahih al-Bukhari*, Hadith no. 2585

applies to anything that would lead others to be similarly upset.

It is improper to take back a gift after giving it or after promising to give it to someone, much like anyone would find eating vomit repulsive. Taking gifts back is offensive and unethical. It is sinful and goes against the teaching of the Prophet Muhammad ﷺ.

27

Writing off Half the Debt

عن كعب بن مالك أنه تقاضى ابن أبي حدرد دينا كان له عليه في
عهد رسول الله صلى الله عليه وسلم في المسجد فارتفعت
أصواتهما حتى سمعها رسول الله صلى الله عليه وسلم وهو في بيته
فخرج إليهما رسول الله صلى الله عليه وسلم حتى كشف سجف
حجرته ونادى كعب بن مالك فقال يا كعب فقال لبيك يا رسول
الله فأشار إليه بيده أن ضع الشطر من دينك قال كعب قد فعلت
يا رسول الله قال رسول الله صلى الله عليه وسلم قم فاقضه

During the lifetime of the Messenger of Allah ﷺ, Ka'b ibn Mālik ؓ reported that he pressed Ibn Abū Ḥadrad in the mosque for the payment of a debt that he owed to him. In this altercation their voices became loud, until Allah's Messenger ﷺ heard them, while he was in the house, so he came out towards them, lifted the curtain of his apartment, and he called upon Ka'b ibn Mālik and said: 'O Ka'b.' He said: 'Yes, O Messenger of Allah.' He gestured with his hand to remit half of the loan due to him. Ka'b said: 'I will do, O Messenger of Allah.' Thereupon Allah's Messenger ﷺ said (to Ibn Abū Ḥadrad): 'Stand up and make him the payment (of the rest).'

Allah has not given everything to any one person to the extent that they can live life without the help of others. Everyone needs the help of someone else on a regular basis. Much like the poor need the help of the rich, the rich need the help of the poor. Borrowing money is one of those regular activities that human beings do. It happens that some people borrow money and then struggle to pay it back and this can stress friendships and spoil relationships.

It is part of human nature to be attached to and concerned about wealth. We are protective over our own wealth, and most of us seek out ways to increase the amount of wealth we have. It is not blameworthy to desire wealth and to work hard to obtain it. It is also not blameworthy to seek out your right when it comes to money, as the noble Companion, Ka'b ibn Mālik ؓ, did in this hadith. That is because justice dictates that people are entitled to request the return of what belongs to them.

When Ka'b ؓ requested the man to return what he owed him while in the Prophet's mosque in Madinah, their voices began to rise. As the Prophet's house was attached to the mosque, he could hear the commotion and came out. The Prophet ﷺ knew Ka'b ؓ was wealthy enough to write off half of the debt, and so he called for Ka'b's attention and told him to waiver half of the debt. The Companions had the greatest love and respect for the Prophet Muhammad ﷺ and they would do anything for him. Ka'b ؓ did not hesitate to immediately relinquish the man for half of what he owed him. The Prophet ﷺ then commanded the man to go and pay off the remaining half.

There are many lessons that we can take away from this hadith. Firstly, Muslims should keep to their promises in returning and receiving money, so that disputes are avoided. Secondly, one should try to be as forgiving and lenient as possible when dealing with financial transactions, just like Ka'b ؓ decided to overlook half of what he was owed. Leniency when buying and selling is a sign that a person has not allowed the love of money to overtake their heart. Instead, it remains in their hand and under their control, so that they are able to use it in the most beneficial way. The Prophet Muhammad ﷺ asked Allah to have mercy on the one who is easy-going when buying, selling, and seeking a debt to be returned.

Ka'b's action was noble and what he gave up was regarded as an act of charity. Every person should assess the person they are lending money to, and if in the future they see that they are genuinely struggling to pay it off, they should try their best to reduce the amount and forgo whatever amount they can so as to make matters easy for the borrower. The lender will not lose out on anything because Allah will return their money to them in full and through means they wouldn't have ever imagined. Allah says in the Qur'an: *'And whatever good you do it is for yourselves, and whatever you spend should be for the sake of Allah, and whatever you give shall be returned back to you and you shall not be wronged'* (*al-Baqarah* 2: 272).

How to Wash the Dead: Death During Hajj

عن ابن عباس رضى الله عنهما عن النبى صلى الله عليه وسلم
خر رجل من بعيره فوقص فمات فقال اغسلوه بماء وسدر وكفنوه
فى ثوبيه ولا تخمروا رأسه فإن الله يبعثه يوم القيامة ملبيا

Ibn 'Abbās ﵄ reported that a person fell down from his camel in *iḥrām*[17] and died. Thereupon the Messenger of Allah ﷺ said: 'Bathe him with water mixed with the leaves of the lote tree, shroud him in his two pieces of cloth, and do not cover his head, for Allah will raise him on the Day of Judgement pronouncing the *talbiyah*[18].'

---

17 Special clothing worn by pilgrims for hajj.

18 A special chant proclaimed during the hajj: The *talbiyah* is: *labbayka-llāhumma labbayka, labbayka lā sharīka laka labbayka, inna-l-ḥamda wa-n-ni'mata laka wa-l-mulka lā sharīka lak* (Here I am [at Your service] O Allah, here I am. Here I am [at Your service]. You have no partners (other gods). To You alone is all praise and all excellence, and to You is all sovereignty. There is no partner to You).

Death is a reality which no one can deny, be they people of faith or no faith. No one knows where or how they will die until their time has come. Some people are fortunate in the sense that Allah gives them notice that their time on Earth is up and they need to put their affairs in order. For others, death comes upon them suddenly and without notice.

This hadith reinforces two things: firstly, that death can come at any time and unexpectedly. Secondly, believers are brothers and sisters. This brotherhood is not one which Muslims are merely encouraged to uphold, rather it is an obligatory article of Islam that has been established in the Qur'an by Allah. Allah says: *'Indeed all believers are brothers'* (*al-Ḥujurāt* 49: 10). This brotherhood, therefore, necessitates that Muslims have rights over one another. One of the rights that a Muslim has over another Muslim is the right to be looked after upon their death. It is a right that every Muslim has upon the community that he or she is washed, prayed upon, buried, and respected during the process. When the deceased is washed, the Prophet Muhammad ﷺ commanded his followers to use *sidr*, a type of plant which gives off a pleasant scent. Similarly, we should use perfumes and other things which ensure that the deceased appears in the best and most pleasant form possible in front of others. This is part of doing that which we would like others to do for us, and it also ensures that people who see the deceased after being washed see them in the best form, which then brings about optimism in the family and friends of the deceased.

The simple manner of washing the deceased can be done by washing any impurities that need to exit the body, and then washing the whole body with water, in no particular sequence or method. However, it is recommended to wash the deceased as per the method taught in the Prophetic Sunnah. That is to ensure that their private parts are covered at all times, to then wash away any impurities, to wash the limbs which one washes during ablution–the face, hands, head, and feet–and then to wash the whole body using water and other cleansing products, such as soap. It is also recommended that only those washing or helping to wash should attend, so that the deceased is respected and covered as much as possible. The deceased should be shrouded and prayed upon before burial.

This hadith teaches us two important lessons. Firstly, the right of the deceased; that is to say, a person should be bathed in the method described above and shrouded. This is a way of honouring the dead.

Secondly, the Prophet ﷺ wanted to teach Muslims what to do when a person dies during hajj and in the state of *iḥrām*, because passing away while in the state of *iḥrām* is a special occurrence and not the same as passing away at other times. The deceased in this case will be honoured in such a way that they will be raised on the Day of Judgement chanting the *talbiyah*. The Prophet ﷺ told the Companions to avoid doing for the deceased that which a person in a state of *iḥrām* would avoid doing themselves, such as covering the head, as the one who passes away in a state of *iḥrām* will be raised up and judged as a pilgrim to Allah's House on the Day of Judgement.

29

An Easy Way to Get the Reward of Reading One-third of the Qur'an

عن أبي الدرداء عن النبي صلى الله عليه وسلم قال أيعجز أحدكم أن يقرأ في ليلة ثلث القرآن؟ قالوا وكيف يقرأ ثلث القرآن؟ قال قل هو الله أحد تعدل ثلث القرآن

Abū ad-Dardā' ﵁ reported that the Messenger of Allah ﷺ said: 'Is any one of you incapable of reciting a third of the Qur'an in a night?' They asked: 'How could one recite a third of the Qur'an in a night?' He replied: '*Say: He Allah is One* (i.e., *Surah al-Ikhlāṣ*)[19] is equivalent to a third of the Qur'an.'

The Qur'an is the Word of Allah, and it is a great blessing and mercy from Allah to His creation. It is a guide which aids us in living an

19 Qur'an surah 112

informed and balanced life in this world, and directs us to salvation in the afterlife. The whole Qur'an is a guidance, just as all the Messengers of Allah were sent to guide people. However, some verses and chapters of the Qur'an are given a special virtue, due to the particularly great meanings they provide. For example, the Prophet Muhammad ﷺ spoke of *Surah al-Fātiḥah* (the opening chapter of the Qur'an) as being the greatest chapter in the Qur'an, and of *Āyat al-Kursī*[20] being the greatest verse in the Qur'an. It is not possible for us to know which verses or surahs have special virtues nor is it permissible for us to make such claims; rather, we are only able to know this through revelation from Allah to the Prophet Muhammad ﷺ. The reason why these verses or surahs have special virtues is connected to the meaning they represent. *Surah al-Ikhlāṣ* solely discusses the greatest attribute of Allah ﷻ His Oneness. The Oneness of Allah (or *tawḥīd* in Arabic) is the most significant element of belief a person must have about Allah. This is the foundation of faith and without it, believing in Allah or anything else is pointless. Knowing this attribute and appreciating its magnificence is a reason for being sincere towards Allah in worship.

At the time of the Prophet Muhammad ﷺ, a man sat down in the early morning before dawn reciting *Surah al-Ikhlāṣ* and kept repeating it. When the Prophet ﷺ was informed about this, he said: 'By Allah it is equal to a third of the Qur'an.'[21] The Prophet Muhammad ﷺ taught his followers the great status of the Qur'an, not only so that we can repeat its recitation, but the regular recitation of this chapter is intended to act as a means of contemplation, comprehension, and living our lives with it in mind.

Here, we must note the difference between two concepts in Islam: namely *jazā'* (rewards) and *ijzā'* (what is sufficient). The hadith explained in this chapter does not imply that one can simply recite

20 See *al-Baqarah* 2: 255

21 Al-Nasa'i, *Sunan al-Nasa'i,* Hadith no. 995

Surah al-Ikhlāṣ three times and consider themselves to have completed the recitation of the whole Qur'an. This is a common misconception. Neither does it take the place of nor does it suffice (*ijzā'*) as the completion of the *muṣḥaf*. Instead, what the hadith indicates is that *Surah al-Ikhlāṣ*, although a short surah, is so profound in its subject matter that reciting it will grant us rewards (*jazā'*) equivalent to those of reciting one-third of the entire Qur'an. Truly, when we contemplate on the meaning of this surah—that there is only One true God, Who has always been, Who never ceases to exist, Who has no equal, and the only One worthy of turning to at all times—it will most certainly have a great impact in our lives and on our view of the world around us.

30

The Virtues of Praying at a Mosque

عن أبى هريرة قال قال رسول الله صلى الله عليه وسلم صلاة الرجل فى جماعة تزيد على صلاته فى بيته وصلاته فى سوقه۞ بضعا وعشرين درجة وذلك أن أحدهم إذا توضأ فأحسن الوضوء ثم أتى المسجد لا ينهزه إلا الصلاة لا يريد إلا الصلاة۞ فلم يخط خطوة إلا رفع له بها درجة وحط عنه بها خطيئة حتى يدخل المسجد فإذا دخل المسجد كان فى الصلاة ما كانت الصلاة هى تحبسه والملائكة يصلون على أحدكم ما دام فى مجلسه الذى صلى فيه يقولون اللهم ارحمه اللهم اغفر له اللهم تب عليه ما لم يؤذ فيه ما لم يحدث فيه

Abū Hurayrah ﵁ reported the Messenger of Allah ﷺ as saying: 'A man's prayer in congregation is better than his prayer in his house and his market by some twenty levels. That is because when he performs ablution excellently, then goes out to the mosque, doing so only for the sake of the prayer, he has no other objective before him but prayer. He does not take a step except that he is raised a degree for it and has a sin remitted for it, until he enters the mosque, and when he is busy in prayer after having entered the mosque, the angels continue to invoke blessing on him as long as he is in his place of worship, saying: "O Allah, show him mercy, and pardon him! Accept his repentance," so long as he does not do any harm in it or loses his ablution.'

Prayer or *Ṣalāh* in Arabic is one of the most significant ways of worshipping Allah. This is because *Ṣalāh* is performed regularly and multiple times in a day. It is a constant reminder about the Oneness of Allah and the reason why Allah created human beings. The best acts of worship are those which are done privately, because they are more likely to be sincere and distant from showing off. This is one reason the Prophet Muhammad ﷺ said the best of prayer is the one performed at home—except the five daily prayers.

There must be a balance between private and collective worship. A society cannot thrive with only private worship where no acts of worship are made collectively, or with collective worship without any private worship being performed by its people. By striking a balance between the two, a stronger and better community is formed.

There are some acts of worship which have greater benefits when done in public. The five daily prayers is an example of such. This is because the five prayers in particular serve a purpose more than to simply worship Allah sincerely. They act as a gathering in which community members are aware of one another, which allows them to work together and support one another. The theme of collective worship is found in all five pillars of Islam. Fasting and pilgrimage are clearly collective acts of worship that have a special ethos to them, and zakat, although less public, is typically one that is arranged and organised by the state for the benefit of the wider community. When good actions become public, it is easier for them to spread in the community, because societal norms have a large impact on our behaviour and our morals. The more people see that the mosques are filled with worshippers, the easier it becomes for them to attend too. These are just some of the fruits of congregational prayers in the mosque; hence the great emphasis on it.

In this hadith, the Prophet Muhammad ﷺ told us that performing the obligatory prayers in congregation is twenty or so times greater than praying individually. Then he explained the proper prayer routine which is worthy of such multiplied rewards by Allah—that is when one perfects their ablution and then walks to the mosque with total concentration on the prayer, and without harming others. The angels then supplicate and pray for that person while they await the prayer, and it is as though they are in prayer while they await it. So, one should not feel that they are wasting time by waiting or get upset that the prayer has been delayed by a few minutes or so while the congregation awaits the imam.

31

Women Attending Mosques

عن ابن عمر أن رسول الله صلى الله عليه وسلم قال لا تمنعوا إماء الله مساجد الله

'Abdullāh ibn Umar ﷺ reported that the Messenger of Allah ﷺ said: 'Do not prevent women from attending the mosques of Allah.'

A community can only be stable when men and women are part of it, and each play a positive role to better themselves and society. Islam emphasises on keeping the community together. This can be clearly seen in the five daily prayers at the mosque, the weekly Friday prayer, Ramadan, Eid, and other communal practices. Regularly attending prayers at the mosque is particularly emphasised because it ensures that a person holds tightly to their prayers at its correct time, and it also reinforces that prayer is a major pillar of Islam. Besides being a religious responsibility, prayer is food for the soul and tonic for righteous consciousness. Without it, a person is missing a part of their soul and their moral compass will struggle to find its bearings.

To worship in the mosque is a right that every Muslim has. Nobody has the right to prevent another Muslim from worshipping Allah and attending the mosque because the mosques do not belong to anyone except Allah. Allah states in the Qur'an: *'And the mosques belong to Allah, so do not call upon anyone besides Allah'* (al-Jinn 72: 18).

In this hadith, the Prophet Muhammad ﷺ specifically prohibited men from preventing women from going to the mosques. During the time of the Prophet ﷺ, it was not uncommon for men to prevent their wives or womenfolk from leaving the house to attend the mosque. The Prophet ﷺ thus explicitly clarified that women also have a right to the mosque, and the noble female Companions would regularly attend prayers at the mosque, including the morning Fajr prayer[22] and the late-night Ishā' prayer.[23]

Although understandable that, out of concern for her safety, a man may not feel comfortable with his wife going out at untimely hours, however, we see that, it should not lead one to oppose the command of the Prophet Muhammad ﷺ. The leader of the believers, Umar ibn al-Khaṭṭāb ؓ, was not so fond of his wife constantly praying in the mosque. When she got to know about this, she told him that she would stop going if he wanted that. However, Umar ؓ refused to prevent her from going, because he knew that the Prophet Muhammad ﷺ gave them this right. Particularly, in times of difficulty and trials, we should encourage men and women to be attached to the mosque, which acts as a connection to Allah and keeps a person away from useless activities that they may otherwise spend their time doing.

It is worth noting that the Prophet Muhammad ﷺ has also stated that a woman's prayer in her home is better than her prayer at a

---

22 Al-Bukhari, *Sahih al-Bukhari*, Hadith no. 372
23 Al-Nasa'i, *Sunan al-Nasa'i*, Hadith no. 5260

mosque.[24] Moreover, due to change of times and norms, some scholars have suggested that it is better for women to pray at home for their own safety. If there is no fear of harm, then no woman should be stopped from attending the mosque for prayer.

24 Abu Dawud, *Sunan Abi Dawud*, Hadith no. 567

Taking a Bath When it's Cold

عن جابر بن عبد الله أن وفد ثقيف سألوا النبي صلى الله عليه وسلم فقالوا إن أرضنا أرض باردة فكيف بالغسل؟ فقال أما أنا فأفرغ على رأسى ثلاثا

Jābir ibn 'Abdullāh ﵁ reported that a delegation from Thaqīf asked the Messenger of Allah ﷺ saying: 'We live in a cold land. What should we do about *ghusl* (ritual bath)?' He said: 'As for me, I pour over my head three times.'

'Indeed, Allah loves those who constantly repent and He loves those who keep themselves pure and clean' (*al-Baqarah* 2: 222).

This is a clear message from Allah about how He regards those who keep clean. Cleanliness and purification are fundamental to Islam and the key to prayer. The daily prayers are very important acts of worship, and therefore, it is essential for every Muslim to learn the rules of prayer in order to ensure that prayer is performed in the most correct way possible.

As stated above, one of the conditions required for prayer to be valid is purification. There are two types of purification for prayer: *wuḍū'* (ablution) and *ghusl* (bath). *Wuḍū'* is required when one is in a minor state of impurity such as after using the toilet or after sleep. *Ghusl* is required when one is in a major state of impurity, such as, following sexual intercourse or menstruation.

Once a group of people came to visit the Prophet Muhammad ﷺ from a place called Thaqīf, not too far from Makkah. In their meeting with him, they told him that they come from a place where it is cold and enquired about performing *ghusl*. The Prophet Muhammad ﷺ responded to them by not giving them a direct command or instruction. Instead, he told them what he did, reminding them that the role model in worshipping Allah is the Prophet himself. The reason for their question was probably that heating water would take a long time, and then when in a state of no clothes except for undergarments, the nippy wind may cause a chill and discomfort for them. So they wanted to know what the minimum requirements for *ghusl* were.

The Prophet Muhammad ﷺ answered them with a simple explanation of the basic version of the ritual bath, as opposed to teaching them about the complete version of it, which the Prophet ﷺ used to regularly perform himself, as reported to us by his wife, 'Ā'ishāh ﵂ and others.

The complete ritual bath of the Prophet ﷺ involves first washing the hands before washing any impurities from the private parts, then performing ablution (*wuḍū'*), and finally washing the whole body by pouring water over the head and washing the right side before the left.[25] However, in cases of cold or limited time, one can simply wash

25 Muslim, *Sahih Muslim*, Hadith no. 618, 620, 619, 616, 623; Abu Dawud, *Sunan Abi Dawud*, Hadith no. 242

themselves by ensuring that the water reaches each part of their body, in no particular order. This is the minimum necessity for ritual bathing (*ghusl*) to be complete.

In cases of severe cold that may lead to illness, it is permissible for one to refrain from having a ritual bath altogether and instead resort to *tayammum* (dry ablution), using soil, sand, stone, or other parts which form the natural surface of the earth to wipe the hands and face. This is a substitute for *wuḍū'* and *ghusl* when water cannot be used.

33

Spending Money

عن جابر أن رسول الله صلى الله عليه وسلم قال ابدأ بنفسك فتصدق عليها فإن فضل شىء فلأهلك فإن فضل عن أهلك شىء فلذى قرابتك فإن فضل عن ذى قرابتك شىء فهكذا وهكذا يقول فبين يديك وعن يمينك وعن شمالك

Jābir ﵁ reported that the Messenger of Allah ﷺ said: 'Start with your own self and spend on yourself. If anything is left, it should be spent on your family. If anything is left (after meeting the needs of the family) it should be spent on relatives. If anything is left after this, it should be spent like this and like this.' And he was saying (i.e., he meant): 'In front of you, on your right and on your left.'

Having money is an important part of human life. Spending money for noble causes is one of the best and most impactful actions anyone can do. This is why the Qur'an is full of verses that command and encourage spending from our wealth. Allah says in the Qur'an about the qualities of a believer: '*Who believe in the unseen, establish prayer, and spend out of what We have provided for them'* (*al-Baqarah* 2: 3).

Spending wealth in good causes, such as educational projects, mosques, hospitals, to support and to gift it to our own family members, and to help those in need, is one of the best ways to purify our hearts and our wealth. This is because it teaches us to spend without being so attached to our wealth. It also helps to purify our wealth of any questionable contamination that may have been out with our control. Allah says in the Qur'an, addressing the Prophet Muhammad ﷺ: *'Take from their wealth a Ṣadaqah (charity) that cleanses and purifies them'* (*al-Tawbah* 9: 10). Along with these teachings, the Qur'an has taught us to remain moderate in the way we spend our wealth, so that we do not end up causing more harm than good or ignoring things which should be prioritised. The Qur'an teaches: *'Do not keep your hand tied to your neck, nor extend it to the full extent, lest you end up sitting reproached, empty handed'* (*al-Isrā'* 17: 29). In other words, do not be miserly, but also do not spend excessively to the extent that you harm yourself or others.

In this hadith, the Prophet Muhammad ﷺ wanted to teach Muslims what to do when they have money and how they should spend it. Here, the Prophet ﷺ advised that one should begin by spending on those they are responsible for, including their own selves. If one does not have that which suffices them and their family, then spending on others would be an incorrect choice. If one has been blessed with enough wealth after providing for themselves and those they are responsible for, then in such a case, the Prophet Muhammad ﷺ told us to spend on our relatives.

Spending money on relatives does not only mean giving them charity. They may not need your money, but they may need your good company and friendship. This means that one should maintain good family ties and regularly invite them to share a meal or do other activities together.

The Prophet ﷺ advised that any surplus money beyond our needs should be spent 'like this and that'. He said that while moving his hands from the right to the left. This phrase means that we should spend without hesitation, because the reward of giving in noble causes is never lost. It brings great blessings to our lives, and we will then see its fruits in the next life.

Fasting While Travelling

عن عائشة رضى الله عنها أنها قالت سأل حمزة بن عمرو
الأسلمى رسول الله صلى الله عليه وسلم عن الصيام فى السفر⬤
فقال إن شئت فصم وإن شئت فأفطر

'Ā'ishah ⬤ said that Ḥamzah ibn 'Amr al-Aslamī ⬤
asked the Messenger of Allah ⬤ about fasting during
travel. He replied: 'If you wish you can fast and if you
wish you may eat.'

Fasting is one of the noblest acts of worship and from the most
beloved deeds to Allah. The Prophet Muhammad ⬤ told us that
Allah rewards those who fast without enumeration. The reason for
this, as Allah says, is because, 'He (man) leaves his food, his drink, and
his human desire, for My sake.'[26]

---

26 Al-Bukhari, *Sahih al-Bukhari*, Hadith no. 7492

Islam teaches balance and moderation and therefore, as with all acts of worship, Islam discourages overburdening oneself. It is a false sense of piety for people to be extreme in worshipping Allah and do things which may harm them. Once the Prophet ﷺ was told by ʿĀ'ishah ؓ about a woman who performed large amounts of prayer and worship, but the Prophet ﷺ was not impressed by that and said: 'Keep to those actions that are within your capability.'[27]

When it comes to the matter of fasting specifically, the Prophet Muhammad ﷺ saw a man who fainted due to fasting while travelling, and so he remarked: 'It is not from piety to fast during travel.'[28] This statement was made in the context of someone who overburdened himself with fasting during travel despite knowing that there is a potential of being harmed by fasting. As for the one who knows that they will most likely not be harmed, then this hadith teaches us that it is acceptable for them to fast.

The Qur'an also talks about fasting whilst travelling and has explicitly given a concession for travellers to break their fast if they wish. Allah says: *'And whoever is ill or on a journey (they may break their fast and) make up for it on other days'* (al-Baqarah 2: 185). In this hadith, the Prophet ﷺ taught a general principle which relates to fasting for a traveller. The Prophet ﷺ himself would often fast while travelling and this hadith explains that travellers can fast if they want to, so long as they do not fear being harmed by fasting.

Although this hadith discusses fasting, it provides us with a recurring principle in the Prophetic teachings—that worship is not intended to be excessive or burdensome, and that we should not opt for options which may cause difficulty, when we have other permissible options available. This applies to acts of specific worship just as much as it applies to our daily life interactions.

---

27 Al-Bukhari, *Sahih al-Bukhari*, Hadith no. 42

28 Al-Bukhari, *Sahih al-Bukhari*, Hadith no. 1946

35

How to Behave While Fasting

عن أبي هريرة رضى الله عنه رواية قال إذا أصبح أحدكم يوما صائما فلا يرفث ولا يجهل فإن امرؤ شاتمه أو قاتله فليقل إني صائم إني صائم

Abū Hurayrah ﷺ reported that the Prophet Muhammad ﷺ said: 'When any one of you gets up in the morning in the state of fasting, he should neither use obscene language nor do any act of ignorance. And if anyone should insult him or quarrel with him, he should say: "I am fasting, I am fasting."'

The most important objective for every Muslim should be to purify the heart. If the heart is pure and sound, then this will be reflected in our actions, as the Prophet Muhammad ﷺ said, 'Behold in your body there is an organ, if that becomes good then the entire body becomes good and if that becomes bad then the entire body becomes bad, and that organ is the heart.'[29] However, a good heart cannot be achieved by simply wanting to do good, rather it becomes good by actually doing good. Praying, fasting, and reciting the Qur'an are all acts of great servitude to Allah, but they are also intended to purify our hearts, which in turn leads us to living an informed and noble life. We should not consider acts of worship to be superficial deeds which are achieved by simply following the rules. Rather, we should view them as essential spiritual actions which bring us closer to Allah, and impact us in our lives.

The main aim of fasting is not for humans to go without food and drink from sunrise to sunset, but instead is to bring a person closer to Allah; and the way a person becomes closer to Allah is by abandoning sinful actions. If a person prays yet lies, or gives charity yet steals, then what benefit has such a person achieved from worshipping Allah? In like manner, fasting is all about teaching self-restraint. Therefore, if a person is fasting yet they fail to restrain their tongue, even if provoked, what benefit of fasting has he or she achieved?

Fasting consists of abandoning food, drink and human desires during the day. If someone does this, they will have fasted from a legal perspective. However, if during the fast, they backbite, hurt others, disrespect their parents, and the like, then they have failed to achieve the true benefits of fasting. Although they would not be required to repeat their fast, they have missed out on the objective of fasting. The Prophet ﷺ said in another hadith: 'Whoever does not leave false speech and acting according to it, and ignorance, then Allah is in no need of them to leave their food and drink.'[30] This is why the Prophet ﷺ told those who are hurt or irritated by others while fasting to respond by saying: 'I am fasting' and not engage in retaliating and responding to

29 Al-Bukhari, *Sahih al-Bukhari*, Hadith no. 52

30 Al-Bukhari, *Sahih al-Bukhari*, Hadith no. 6057

the abuse. By doing this, it acts as a reminder to ourselves to keep away from anything which may damage the purpose of our fast, and it serves as a reminder to others to refrain from instigating a fasting person.

A true fast is one which is free from sin, harming others, and false speech. The same is to be said about other acts of worship, such as hajj. The Prophet ﷺ said: 'Whoever performs hajj, and does not fall into false speech and sin, will return like the day his mother gave birth to him.' This is the kind of hajj and fast which bears its fruits, and this ought to be our mentality in all our acts of worship; that they are to be done with excellence.

36

The Virtue of Ashura

عن عائشة رضى الله عنها قالت كانت قريش تصوم عاشوراء فى الجاهلية وكان رسول الله صلى الله عليه وسلم يصومه فلما هاجر إلى المدينة صامه وأمر بصيامه فلما فرض شهر رمضان قال من شاء صامه ومن شاء تركه

'Ā'ishah ﵂ reported that the Quraysh used to fast on the day of Ashura in the pre-Islamic days and the Prophet ﷺ also observed it. When he migrated to Madinah, he himself observed this fast and commanded others to observe it. But when fasting during the month of Ramadan was made obligatory, he said: 'He who wishes to observe this fast may do so, and he who wishes to abandon it may do so.'

The month of Muharram is one of the four sacred months that the Qur'an has alluded to. There are many virtues to this month, which is why the Prophet ﷺ encouraged fasting during this month. He said, 'The best fast after the fast of Ramadan is that which is in the month of Allah; Muharram.'[31] It is therefore recommended to fast during this month. However, special significance is given to the 10th day of this month, known as the day of Ashura. This day was so significant that even the polytheists in the pre-Islamic era would fast this day. Perhaps this was something they took from the Jews.

The Prophet ﷺ would fast on this day even after migrating to Madinah and he encouraged the Muslims to fast too. When Ramadan was legislated in the second year after the Hijrah (migration to Madinah), fasting the day of Ashura no longer held the same emphasis. Some of the Companions, such as 'Abdullāh ibn Mas'ūd ؓ, stopped fasting Ashura after the legislation of Ramadan. Nonetheless, it was still something that would be observed by many Muslims.

When the Prophet ﷺ asked the Jews about their fasting on the day of Ashura, they explained that this was a great day of celebration for them on which Allah had saved Moses ؑ from Pharaoh. Upon hearing this, the Prophet ﷺ said, 'We are more deserving of Moses than you.'[32] What he meant was that the Muslims are closer followers of Prophet Mūsā ؑ than the Jews are, because they follow the true teachings of Mūsā ؑ. He then commanded the Muslims to fast it.

Therefore, since the early times, Muslims continued to fast the day of Ashura. The Prophet Muhammad ﷺ told us that fasting the day of Ashura wipes away the sins of the previous year. Fasting the day of Ashura is hence recommended, even if this is fasted alone or if it coincides with Friday or Saturday. However, the Prophet ﷺ did make his intention clear to fast the 9th as well as the 10th of Muharram, so as

---

31 Al-Nasa'i, *Sunan al-Nasa'i,* Hadith no. 1613

32 Al-Bukhari, *Sahih al-Bukhari,* Hadith no. 2004

to be different from the Jews. He said, 'If I am alive the following year, I would fast the ninth.'[33] However, he passed away before this happened. For this reason, most scholars recommend fasting both the 9th and 10th of Muharram, although fasting the 10th alone is permissible.

33 Muslim, *Sahih Muslim*, Hadith no. 1134

37

A Bad Haircut

عن ابن عمر أن رسول الله صلى الله عليه وسلم نهى عن القزع قال قلت لنافع وما القزع قال يحلق بعض رأس الصبى ويترك بعض

Ibn Umar ﷺ reported that the Messenger of Allah ﷺ forbade *qaza'*. It was said to Nāfi': 'What is *qaza'*?' He said: 'To shave a part of a boy's head and to leave a part unshaven.'

Beauty and keeping a presentable appearance are certainly praiseworthy things. Keeping a good appearance makes us more content with ourselves, gives us confidence, and a sense of self-respect. It also makes others around us more comfortable with us and is something beloved to Allah. In another hadith, the Prophet ﷺ said: 'Allah is beautiful and loves beauty.'[34] At the same time, Islam teaches us

34 Muslim, *Sahih Muslim,* Hadith no. 1659

to remain balanced and well-proportioned with our appearance, so that beauty and appearance are not taken to extreme lengths. This is why the Prophet ﷺ prohibited certain extreme changes to the body, such as applying tattoos, false hair, mutilation of body parts and anything which causes disfigurement. Similarly, the Prophet Muhammad ﷺ prohibited men from imitating women and women from imitating men. This is mainly because it causes the natural appearance and features of men and women to be altered and damaged, while Islam came to take men and women towards their most complete nature, spiritually and physically.

Although Islam finds beauty and looking sharp laudable it has set guidelines and boundaries for lawful types of beauty and fashion. Grooming and fashioning our hair is very important because it represents a very important aspect of our looks and appearance. However, this hadith shows that it is discouraged for men to have exaggerated haircuts which may contradict good etiquette, looking presentable, and keeping an appropriate balance in our appearance. This is the general objective behind the discouragement of what this hadith refers to as *qazaʿ*.

When it comes to detailing what exactly is meant by *qazaʿ*, there are some varying interpretations held by jurists. Many jurists only discourage completely shaving part of the head and keeping another part. Doing so is disliked according to the majority of scholars. Based on this, there is no problem in keeping different hair lengths, such as the sides being shorter than the top. This is how the hadith was interpreted by Nāfiʿ, who was the student of the illustrious Companion and the narrator of this hadith, ʿAbdullāh ibn Umar ﷺ. This is also the view of Imam Aḥmad ibn Ḥanbal and other leading jurists. However, once again, all this should be done while keeping in mind the respectable and appropriate balance that the Sunnah encourages, and whilst avoiding excesses, particularly those which make a person stand out and appear odd in the eyes of people.

Breastfeeding a Child

عن عائشة قالت قال لى رسول الله صلى الله عليه وسلم يحرم
من الرضاعة ما يحرم من الولادة

'Ā'ishah ❀ reported that the Messenger of Allah ❀ said:
'Breastfeeding a child makes unlawful what giving birth
makes unlawful.'

It is from the mercy of Allah that He filled the breasts of our
mothers with milk as food for us when we were born. Unable to eat
any types of solid food, milk was the only sustenance which kept us
alive. The Arabs had a custom of employing wet-nurses to breastfeed
children. Islam dictates that this, i.e., breastfeeding, establishes a special
bond between the child and the wet-nurse, namely that of a foster
relationship. Islam gives this bond great importance and value.

The protection of family is a major objective in Islam. Many of
the rulings and teachings contained in the Qur'an came with the aim

of building and keeping the family stable and preserving the lineage of people. A strong family system ensures the stability of society and leads to good upbringing of children. This is why Islam has forbidden cutting family ties.

What constitutes a familial relationship comes at varying levels. Parents, uncles, and cousins are all family members in broad terms. However, some are clearly closer than others. Islam has also made breastfeeding a cause of family relations. This means that the foster child becomes like a child the wet-nurse gave birth to. For example, if a girl was breastfed by a woman, then she becomes like a sister to that woman's children, a daughter to her husband and a granddaughter to her parents. This means that marriage is not permissible between them, the same as the children she gave birth to. Furthermore, all other rulings related to a child of blood such as hijab, travelling with them and the like, applies to a foster child as well. In effect, she is exactly like a girl the wet-nurse gave birth to when it comes to matters of prohibition.

There is, however, one exception to this rule and that is related to inheritance. Although all the rules of a blood-child apply to a child fed by breast milk, the child cannot inherit from her milk-mother and her family. So, the girl in the example above would not inherit from her foster parents and she would keep the name of her biological father. If her milk-parent wishes to give her something from their estate, they are allowed to bequeath something for her, but unlike the blood-child, the milk-children do not inherit automatically from the milk-parents.

There are many benefits including health benefits of breastfeeding. As we just saw, Islam has encouraged breastfeeding to the extent that it has made it a cause of establishing family relations similar to blood relations. However, this relationship is established only if breastfeeding occurs within the first two years[35] of the child and with a minimum

---

35 Some say two and half years.

of five complete suckling[36]. If a child is breastfed beyond that time, then the relationship is not established. Breastfeeding is a natural form of feeding a child at a sensitive phase, and one which brings about psychological and emotional benefits, as well as physical ones. Parents are therefore encouraged to give it the attention it deserves and minimise the use of less natural foods, except in cases of need or illness.

36 Al-Nasa'i, *Sunan al-Nasa'i,* Hadith no. 3307

39

The Rights of a Business Partner

عن جابر قال قال رسول الله صلى الله عليه وسلم من كان له شريك فى ربعة أو نخل فليس له أن يبيع حتى يؤذن شريكه فإن رضى أخذ وإن كره ترك

Jābir ibn ʿAbdullāh ﵁ reported the Messenger of Allah ﷺ as saying: 'He who has a partner in a dwelling or a garden, it is not lawful for him to sell that until he is permitted by his partner. If he (the partner) agrees, he should go ahead with it (the sale), and if he disapproves of that, he should abandon it.'

Making profit is a noble goal to aim for if one intends to use the wealth they earn in good ways. However, one should not make money a target to be obtained at the expense of brotherhood, respect, and honesty. There are many examples in the Hadith collections, of financial transactions which the Prophet Muhammad ﷺ did not allow, because they would be a likely cause of dispute and of relations being cut and friendships being broken.

This hadith discusses an important ruling that relates to those who are involved in a business partnership. If two people share a property, for example, and one of the partners wants to sell their share of the property, then they must first offer it to the other partner. If the partner agrees to buy it, then they have more of a right to it, even if a third person made an offer first. This is because partnership involves a relationship of trust and support.

Let's look at it by example. Let's say, partner A sells his share to a third person who is not trustworthy, difficult to deal with, or not so capable of making profit. This would end up causing harm to partner B, because he now has a business partnership with someone who may harm him. It is therefore obligatory for partner A to first inform partner B that he wishes to sell his share to another person, so that partner B can decide whether to buy partner A's share or whether he is happy for the initial sale to go ahead.

This ruling teaches an important etiquette that relates to working with people in business, but it can also be applied to other similar situations that involve sharing things with others, such as our neighbours. If a person wishes to make changes that may affect the neighbours, then they should first seek permission from them. For example, if a person wishes to build an extension to their house and the extension, either due to height or length, may cause inconvenience to their neighbour, then they must be consulted and their permission sought. This shows respect and valuing the close relationship that exists between neighbours, and ensures that no harm is inflicted or reciprocated.

40

Leaving the Mosque after the Call to Prayer

عن أبي الشعثاء قال كنا قعودا فى المسجد مع أبي هريرة فأذن المؤذن فقام رجل من المسجد يمشى فأتبعه أبو هريرة بصره حتى خرج من المسجد فقال أبو هريرة أما هذا فقد عصى أبا القاسم صلى الله عليه وسلم

Abū al-Sha'thā' reported: 'We were sitting with Abū Hurayrah ﵁ in the mosque when the muezzin proclaimed the *adhān*. A man stood up in the mosque and started walking out. Abū Hurayrah stared at him till he went out of the mosque. Upon this Abū Hurayrah said: "Indeed, this man has disobeyed Abul-Qāsim."'

The congregational prayer in the mosque is a greatly significant symbol in Islam. There are several ahadith which talk about its importance, and some scholars like Abū Ḥanīfah, took a very strict opinion regarding offering prayers in congregation. When the call to prayer is made, Muslims are encouraged to proceed to the prayer and to put aside anything which distracts them from that. In *Surah al-Jumu'ah*, Allah says: *'O you who believe, if the call to prayer is made on Friday, then hasten towards the remembrance of Allah, and leave off trade. That is much better for you, if you but know'* (*al-Jumu'ah* 62: 9). The Prophet Muhammad ﷺ felt very strongly about people missing prayer in congregation. It is reported that he said that he would like to have burnt the houses of those who failed to attend the congregational prayer without an excuse.[37]

In this narration, Abū Hurayrah ؓ explains that the Prophet Muhammad ﷺ taught the Companions that once a person is in the mosque after the call to prayer has been made, he should not leave until he has prayed. Of course, if someone had to leave for an emergency or something which cannot be delayed, then he is excused. However, doing so without a valid reason is blameworthy as it indicates a lack of concern for answering the call to prayer and a disregard to the sanctity of the *jamā'ah* (congregation). This is the reason that led Abū Hurayrah ؓ to calling it an act of disobedience.

Leaving the mosque after the prayer has been called may also cause others to think ill of that person. However, as with most rulings, if there is a genuine need, then they are permitted to leave, for such things as appointments which they cannot delay, and so on. Similarly, a person is permitted leave if they wish to catch the prayer at another mosque that is more local to them for instance, if they know that they will make it in time. This is because the objective is that one responds to the call to prayer, so doing so in any mosque is acceptable. Although, remaining in the same mosque and making use of time while waiting for the prayer would be much better, because the Prophet Muhammad ﷺ told us that one is in a state of prayer as long as they await the prayer.

---

37 Muslim, *Sahih Muslim,* Hadith no. 651

This hadith teaches a very important lesson about doing anything which disobeys the teachings of the Prophet Muhammad ﷺ. Pleasing Allah and attaining salvation can only be achieved by following the teachings of the Prophet Muhammad ﷺ, and by doing that we can achieve the ultimate reward of Jannah (Paradise).